# Real Men Cook

## Rites, Rituals, and Recipes for Living

Karega Kofi Moyo

A FIRESIDE BOOK
Published by Simon & Schuster
New York   London   Toronto   Sydney

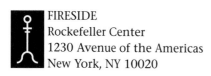

FIRESIDE
Rockefeller Center
1230 Avenue of the Americas
New York, NY 10020

For information regarding special discounts for bulk purchases,
please contact Simon & Schuster Special Sales:
1-800-456-6798 or business@simonandschuster.com

Designed by Charles Kreloff

Manufactured in the United States of America

10   9   8   7   6   5   4   3   2   1

Library of Congress Cataloging-in-Publication Data
    Moyo, Karega, Kofi, 1939–   .
      Real men cook : rites, rituals, and recipes for living / Karega Kofi Moyo.
      p.   cm.
      "A Fireside Book."
      Includes index.
    1. Cookery, American.   2. African American cooks.   I. Title.
      TX715.M9187   2005
641.597—dc22
2005042636

ISBN 0-7432-7242-0

# Contents

# Introduction

**Dedicated to the expression of that inner voice of the Real Man in our midst: the fathers, uncles, brothers, and other men who give "flava to your life."**

Real Men Cook is the longest-running urban Father's Day celebration in America, featuring some of the finest men this nation has ever produced. Every year nearly one thousand men in cities across the United States give up a Sunday of leisure to stand on their feet and feed thousands in the name of charity.

They include men who are single, married, divorced; men who are fathers, coaches, politicians, painters, and entrepreneurs. The food served at Real Men Cook reflects the spiritual essence of men from Chi-town (up-South from Mississippi and Arkansas), N'awlins, Motown, Dallas, D.C., Miami, Philly, L.A., the Big Apple (with fried fish and biscuits on the side), and Hotlanta. But as different as they and the food they cook are, the men all share one thing in common: a commitment to the culture of food and family, community, school, and church, and a love and lust for life.

Increasingly, there is a divide in understanding between men and women, mostly owing to media that often characterize men in negative terms. African American men in particular are often portrayed as criminals, drug addicts, absentee fathers, and jailbirds. Seldom are they depicted as defenders, providers, helpmates, and companions. On the flip side, women and children are given the roles of perpetual victims. This picture is flawed. It fails to recognize the millions of everyday men who strive constantly to make their world, and the world at large, a better place.

That's part of why I, with my wife, Yvette, founded Real Men Cook. It is a crusade to build families and celebrate the Real Men who are often overlooked for their great deeds, mentoring, coaching, and doing their best against the odds of urban life. Can an event change the world? I'm not sure. But year by year, myths are destroyed, hope is restored, perspectives are repositioned, appreciation is expressed, examples are magnified, young men strive to be Real Men, and mature men stand up to be counted; families, no matter the configuration, begin to celebrate themselves and those who try to make a difference.

Some might ask why we chose something like cooking. Why cooking? In the "traditional" way of thinking, cooking is a nurturing activity, and nurturance is an attribute that is not commonly associated with maleness or manliness. Well, I beg to differ. No longer a hunter or defender of the village, modern man has been forced to adapt. Although he is able to exercise his traditional sensibilities on the basketball courts and other fields of physical competition, his repertoire has extended into the more refined realms of music, art, and dance. He has become "civilized," taking on the role of nurturer with unmitigated aplomb.

The Real Man, the modern man, is one who takes things very seriously and doesn't back down from the opinions he holds dear to his heart. He is a man who loves his family, adores his children, enthrones the women in his life, and cherishes his friends. He is a man not unlike so many others he knows, certainly the ones who have elevated Real Men Cook to the level of a veritable social movement; he is a "missionary of culture."

This book is the culmination of a lifetime of discovery, a collection of my personal thoughts, reminiscences, and memories, as well as a compendium of discussions and interviews that relate to food. It is a celebration of men who, like me, "do it in the kitchen" and everywhere else, given the time and opportunity.

I've dedicated the book, first and foremost, to my family. To say that it is "extended" would be an understatement! They are my inspiration for everything that I do.

To begin at the beginning, I owe a great debt of gratitude to my mother, Lydia Louise Monia; my father, Arnold C. Saunders; my maternal grandparents, Walter and Bessie Moore; and Grandpa Hillary and all of the ancestors who made a way for new generations.

I also have to thank Carolyn, Kimya, and Thembi—the mothers of my children—and Yvette, my wife and business partner. They are all capable, strong, and enduring women. As with all mothers, especially black mothers, it is they who have maintained the legacy and heritage of our race and culture.

Most especially, I have to pay homage to my nine beautiful children. Birthdays, graduations, our first wedding, and the coming of our second grandchild have all provided me with opportunities to be part of the common thread of inspiration that gave birth to Real Men Cook for Charity and binds all of the men together.

Above and beyond acknowledging family, this book is an attempt to express gratitude to the hundreds of men who were there when Real Men Cook began sixteen years ago in Chicago. Our thanks extend now to the thousands of men from coast to coast who have since joined our ranks. To all the men whose stories did not make it into this book, do not despair. You were not forgotten, your contributions have been invaluable, and we look forward to hearing your voices in our next book.

W.E.B. DuBois once said, "The Negro race, like all others, is going to be saved by its exceptional men." It is my belief that we are more likely to find that salvation over a plate of tantalizing food, cuisine that feeds our bodies, souls, spirits, and communities with a nutritional value that can neither be underestimated nor accurately measured.

Please listen with all your senses. Hear and taste this!

# Real Men Cook

# CHAPTER ONE

# Tender Gravy

I was blessed to be part of a family in which essential life skills were not relegated to a specific class or gender. Both my father, Arnold Saunders, and my mother, Lydia, could cook, clean, sew, iron, work, make things with their hands, and provide discipline.

A great cook of simple fare, my father frequently made something he called "tender gravy." It was made from the juices of meat, augmented with flour, water, and seasonings, simmered long and ever so slowly to ensure that every grain of flour was saturated. The mixture became tender and somehow much more than the sum of its parts. Even the toughest cuts of meat, fowl, or wild game were completely tenderized and would melt in your mouth. That gravy was served over the meat and the potatoes on the side. What was left could be sopped up with a piece of bread until the plate was shining clean. My father's gravy provides a metaphor for all of the lessons he taught me, lessons that enabled me to grow into manhood with positive values intact and to pass those values on to my own children.

Growing up as I did with parents who took cooking, eating, and nurturing seriously, it's no wonder why I would choose to involve myself for the past sixteen years in an event that challenges preconceptions by elevating men, celebrating families and supporting the community. Real Men Cook is an expression of everything I am and something that I could not help wanting to share with other men of like mind.

Beyond my ambitions for social relevance, there were even more primordial concerns that drove my interest in the event. First and foremost, *I love food,* and I am fascinated by the food industry. My curiosity extends from the garden or farm all the way to the pot on the stove. I can wander around all day in wholesale produce markets where rail and trucks deposit the lifeblood of urban existence. Ethnic markets and groceries that reflect the diversity of American society make city living incredibly exciting to me.

I am humbled by the endless variety of vegetables; the colors, textures, and smells of exotic spices, dried meats, salted fish, and olives; and the various oils infused with herbs and spices for cooking and flavoring. The conversations of the shoppers and, often, the engagement of shop owners as they offer suggestions and personal experiences from their cultural backgrounds are music to my ears. Street markets with thousands of delis and cut flowers invigorate me. I never cease to be amazed by a farming system that ranges from environmentally correct to genetically efficient, a system that churns out questionably nutritious end products that enable millions of Americans to become grossly overfed. As I wander, I wonder, "How does a prepackaged salad get to be *more* expensive than the cost of the separate ingredients of which it is composed? How has 'fresh frozen' emerged as a standard of quality that eclipses what is available at the farmer's market?" In any case, I am awed by the experience.

Secondly, I am motivated no less by the fact that *I love to eat.*

After an early childhood of being thin and sickly with frequent colds and upper respiratory ailments and enduring the relatives who made me eat a multitude of things that I deemed unfit for human consumption, I blossomed into an overachiever in all things edible. Now, fortunately or unfortunately, I have evolved into a person who sees food as something more than just fuel to keep the body going. It is a thing to be experienced, savored, and shared.

"Tender Gravy" emotes the fundamentals of historical cooking and family traditions, and reflects the relationships that these men had with their grandfathers, fathers, or elders who helped shape and mentor them into the men they are today.

The world in which we live is much more diverse than ever before. Its values and views defy the imagination of a man like me, with more than sixty-five years elapsed on my calendar. The "traditional family" of the twenty-first century almost defies definition. We have blended, extended, adoptive, and foster families. Sometimes the mother alone is the head of the household. Increasingly, a father or grandparent is raising the children solo.

No matter what the family configuration, *balance* is required for the best end product. As a rule, children benefit most from the presence of both a mother and father. That was the model I was exposed to growing up, and it is the model that has worked for me in raising nine children, even though we all did not always live in the same household.

Children need help to navigate modernity with all of its conflicts and contradictions. Modern life moves at a disorienting, quick pace: communication, transportation, and forms of entertainment are pushing the limits of what is socially acceptable. The impact of modernity on our families is a subject for another book. Right now, I am merely admonishing readers to sit up and pay attention. Patch up your relationships. Turn off those talk shows. Stop going to the moral court for answers when the real ones are in your heart of hearts. You might have forgotten how or why you found your way to the bedroom, or wherever it was that you *mutually* consented to let "it" happen. The fact remains that "it" happened, and *both* people need to be there for the child that was born as a result. No one can deny that successful adults are ones who benefited from a secure environment while growing up. There were grown-ups in their life who directed their development.

Looking back on my childhood, I realize that my family life was certainly not perfect. Truth is, my parents separated and divorced after twenty-one years of marriage. Many of the issues that led up to the big divide were there for all to see, but the fact remains that *both* of my parents were always supportive of me.

All of the recipes in this section reflect a special relationship and bond that these Real Men had with that uncle, grandfather, father, or elder who took the time to guide these men along the path called life. I have chosen these recipes on purpose. Some were my father's favorites, like Lamb Da-Ra-Ja, and Captain Leander Carter's Famous Chesapeake Bay Fish Chowder. Aside from the fact that my father loved chowders, the recipe connects Stephen Carter with his roots, his grandfather. These recipes established key relationships for these strong brothers who are carrying the torch—and showcasing the positive images of African American men.

# Cooking Is a Sacred Art Form of Reciprocity

Cooking is an art form performed by cultivated givers. It is a culture of sharing. Cooking mixes chemical elements into a healing portion to restore, nurture, and develop the body, mind, and soul of those who ingest it. From an African perspective, the finished product is called "soul food" because it gives enlightenment to the soul as it feeds, nurtures, restores, and mends the hungry, ailing body.

In this light, cooking is a sacred art form. It spiritually connects the cooker and the eater of the food to its divine source and satiates the body and soul with love. It is a love offering that makes them whole and one in the spirit.

Real Men Cook is a sacred venture by sacred men. This is what defines them as Real Men. Real Men are cultivated men. This means that they have been exposed to mentors, and teachers who have taught them the art of culinary science. More important, they have submitted to the wisdom of an elder who in the spirit of reciprocity has given back the gift he has received and passed it on to another Real Man, and in this cycle of giving and receiving, receiving and giving, the circle of love and providence is kept alive.

Real Men Cook is a day of family unity and redemption. It is a day that removes I and Me and unites Us and We. It is a day when the men redeem hunger, thirst, need, and desire. Most of all it is a day of affirmation and restoration, of family, village life, and values.

Real Men Cook is Real Men reaffirming themselves as men being in place, standing tall, providing for their families and the extended family, and reassuring them that their mouths, bodies, and souls will always be full of the grace of a caring father and a gracious, loving God.

Thanks to my mother, my mentor and love, I am proud to be a Real Man who is cultivated to cook with flavor and grace.

*by Morris F. X. Jeff, Jr., Ph.D.*

**Morris F. X. Jeff, Jr., now deceased, was a director of the Department of Human Resources of the city of New Orleans.**

# Andrew J. Williams
# Braised Beef Tenderloin

Andrew J. Williams and
Kofi Moyo

"**F**ood service and hospitality go way back in my family. When my parents married, my mom 'couldn't boil water,' so when my father bought a hotel in Grand Rapids, Michigan, he put her in the kitchen with the chefs. It was the third-largest hotel in Grand Rapids, a great furniture-manufacturing city from the early 1920s until the big crash in 1929. As a result of working with those chefs, she became a fantastic cook, eventually running a successful catering business in Chicago. I worked with her to hone my culinary skills.

"My father was a former All-American football player at Rutgers, a few years behind the legendary Paul Robeson. Dad even played some semipro football with Robeson. I went in another direction altogether, becoming a metallurgical engineer."

**INGREDIENTS**

3 pounds beef tenderloin

1 tablespoon kosher salt

3 tablespoons black pepper

2 tablespoons garlic powder

¼ cup vegetable oil

1 tablespoon dried oregano

2 tablespoons butter, melted

2 cups carrots, cut into chunks on the diagonal

2 onions, cut into quarters

1 cup red dry wine

1. Preheat the oven to 400°F.

2. Season the beef on both sides with the salt, pepper, and garlic powder. Heat a large heavy-bottomed skillet or Dutch oven over medium-high heat. Heat the oil in the skillet for 1 minute, then add the oregano and butter. Place the beef in the skillet and brown on both sides, about 8 minutes total. Add the carrots and onions.

3. Transfer the skillet to the oven, cover, and cook for 20 minutes. Insert a meat thermometer into the center of the beef; it should read medium rare (around 130°F). Remove the tenderloin and vegetables from the skillet, place them on some aluminum foil, and set aside to cool for about 10 minutes. Over medium heat, combine the drippings in the skillet with the wine to make a gravy, scraping up all the bits from the bottom of the pan.

Serves 8

**Andrew J. Williams is a member of the Breakfast Club at the South Side YMCA in Chicago. He is eighty years young, married again, and is still teaching a wife how to cook!!**

## Arthur E. Teele

# Miami Conch Fritters

**INGREDIENTS**

4 pounds fresh conch, diced

2 cups diced celery

3 cups diced green bell pepper

3 cups diced onion

4 hot peppers (bird or scotch bonnet), seeded and diced

8 cups flour

¼ cup baking powder

3 tablespoons tomato paste

1 tablespoon fresh thyme

8 cups vegetable oil

This recipe is from Miami City Councilman Arthur Teele, who is of Bahamian descent. You know those beautiful large shells that you find on the beach and you put them up to your ear and you can hear the sound of the ocean? Well, those beautiful, brightly colored shells are home to the conch. This gastropod mollusk is found primarily in southern waters, and is a very popular dish made several ways in the Caribbean and in Florida.

1. Place the conch, celery, green pepper, onion, and hot peppers into a large bowl. Add the flour, baking powder, tomato paste, thyme, and 4 cups water. Mix together well with a large spoon.

2. Heat the oil in a large saucepan. Using a 2-ounce ice cream scoop, drop the batter into the hot oil and cook until golden. Drain on paper towels.

Makes about 50 fritters

## Bruce Rush
# Big Daddy's Fruit Salad

INGREDIENTS

2 large cantaloupes, cut into cubes

1 large honeydew melon, cut into cubes

1 large pineapple, cut into cubes

2 or 3 apples, cut into small wedges

2 or 3 pears, cut into small wedges

1 large grapefruit, each section cut into 2 or 3 pieces

2 or 3 oranges, each section cut into 2 or 3 pieces (tangerines may be substituted)

12 dried apricots, cut into quarters

¼ pound grapes (preferably seedless)

12 walnuts, shelled and broken into pieces (almonds may be substituted)

3 or 4 bananas, sliced

Three to five 8-ounce containers lemon-flavored yogurt (preferably Dannon's Lemon Chiffon)

Fruit is so important to our diet. All of the fruits listed in this recipe carry key vitamins that are necessary for us to maintain good health. This salad is very easy to make and can be eaten any time of the day.

Combine all of the ingredients except the yogurt, putting the banana slices on top. When ready to serve, top the fruit salad with the yogurt.

Serves 12 to 15

Bruce Rush; his mother, Barbara Summers Rush; and his father, Harold Lee Rush

Frank C. Chaplin

# Creole Cabbage

**INGREDIENTS**

2 medium green cabbages, about 2½ pounds each

1 pound andouille sausage

1 pound smoked sausage

1 pound Mississippi red sausage (rosette)

1 pound bacon

3 cups chopped red bell pepper

2 large onions, cut into ¼-inch slices, slices cut in half

2 cups chopped celery

¼ cup Creole seasoning

¼ cup greens seasoning

1. Cut the cabbages into medium slices. Cut the sausages into silver-dollar slices and sauté in a large pan until done. Remove the cooked sausage from the skillet; reserve the drippings.

2. Cook the bacon in the skillet until crisp and crumbly. Add the cabbage, pepper, onions, and celery to the bacon drippings. Return the sausage to the pan, stir in the Creole and greens seasonings, and cook until the vegetables turn soft.

Serves 6

Kofi Moyo

# Captain Kofi's Candlelight Catfish

**INGREDIENTS**

1 whole catfish (1 to 2 pounds) or catfish steaks (about 1½ inches thick) (If you are going to use catfish steaks, it's important to keep the bone in as the flesh of the fish becomes very soft during cooking. Using a wire basket also helps.)

½ cup olive oil

½ cup soy sauce

½ cup fresh lemon or lime juice

½ cup Italian seasoning

1 teaspoon Old Bay seasoning

½ teaspoon ground cumin

1 tablespoon hot curry powder

¼ to ½ teaspoon cayenne pepper, or to taste

½ teaspoon crushed red pepper flakes

½ tablespoon toasted fennel seeds

In June 1992, as we prepared for our annual radio promotion campaign for Real Men Cook, one of our more prolific and consistent cooks was called into service elsewhere. Pressed by family and friends (and fear of failure) to save the day (or night), Sea Captain Kofi reluctantly stepped in to fill the void. Just as our fearless captain prepared for his maiden voyage as cook for the annual Real Men Cook charity event, Mother Nature intervened with one of the worst late-spring thunderstorms. Lightning struck a transformer and left the harbor in total darkness for thirty-six hours. Undaunted, Captain Kofi found a safe bay under the porch, and with the aid of candlelight began the process of smoking what has now become the legendary Captain Kofi's Candlelight Catfish.

Now, don't let us "smoke" you, but unless you really know your way around the barbie, don't think you can duplicate this voyage alone. Otherwise your catch might be "the one that got away," burnt, dried out, fit to be buried at sea.

1. Clean the fish (leave the bone in). Combine the remaining ingredients and rub into the fish. Let marinate overnight in the refrigerator.

2. Heat the grill to medium heat. Put the fish on, cover, and cook for 15 minutes. Carefully, using a broad spatula, turn the fish over and continue to cook, covered, for 20 to 30 minutes (depending on the thickness).

Serves 4 to 6

Lawrence Ellison

# Savory Oyster Bread Pudding

**INGREDIENTS**

5 cups cubes cut from stale French bread or stale white bread

1 tablespoon salt

Two 12-ounce cans evaporated milk

6 eggs, beaten

¼ pound (1 stick) butter or margarine, softened

6 ounces fresh oysters

Bread pudding is usually a sweet dessert made with slices of bread, eggs, and sometimes chopped fruit. Lawrence Ellison creates a new version of this southern favorite. This is a regional dish, using only the freshest oysters. If fresh oysters are not available, substitute giblets. Serve this side dish with roast turkey, baked ribeye steak, or braised beef tenderloin. It will become a family tradition.

1. Preheat the oven to 350°F.

2. In a large bowl, sprinkle the bread cubes with the salt and moisten with the evaporated milk and 1 cup water. Add the eggs and butter to the bread mixture and stir well. Gently add the oysters (try not to break them apart). Pour the mixture into a 13 by 9-inch baking pan. Bake for 30 to 40 minutes.

Serves 6

## Milton Smith

# Real Greens with Sweet Meat

**INGREDIENTS**

1 pound smoked ribs

1 pound smoked sweet meat (use any smoked meat close to the bone)

2 garlic cloves, chopped

¼ cup crushed red pepper flakes

5 pounds mustard greens

5 pounds turnip greens

Milton Smith has participated with Real Men Cook for thirteen years. His devotion and dedication to the community and his fellow Real Men Cook brothers is an inspiration to all of us.

1. Put the smoked meats into a medium pot and add water to cover. Add the garlic and red pepper flakes. Cook over medium heat for about 1 hour, or until the meat is three-quarters done.

2. Rinse the greens under cold running water three times to remove any sand and grit. Place the greens into a medium pot and pour the hot meat and stock over them. Simmer, covered, over medium heat for 30 minutes or until the greens are cooked to desired tenderness.

Serves 6 to 8

Ozzie Baudin

# Polynesian Meatloaf

## INGREDIENTS

1 pound ground beef

1 pound ground pork

1 teaspoon paprika

2 tablespoons oyster sauce

½ teaspoon salt

1 tablespoon dark brown sugar

⅛ teaspoon black pepper

2 eggs, beaten

½ cup coarse plain bread crumbs

¼ cup soy sauce

4 garlic cloves, minced

1 cup chopped onion

Every family has its own recipe for meatloaf. For a new taste, try this recipe. It includes a few extra flavors that take this old standby to another level. As a matter of fact, make two meatloaves while you're at it. One is to eat now, and the other is for after those long days at work when you don't feel like cooking. Serve it with rice.

1. Preheat the oven to 375°F.

2. Combine all of the ingredients and mix well. Line a 9 by 5 by 3-inch loaf pan with aluminum foil; oil. Shape the meat mixture with your hands into an oval loaf shape. Place in the pan, smooth it out, and bake for 1 hour.

Serves 6 to 8

Peter Henderson

# Buffalo Soldiers' Stampede Stew

"**M**y grandfather was a Buffalo Soldier. I share his memory through this story."

## The Story of the Buffalo Soldiers

Over 180,000 African-Americans served in the Union Army during the Civil War. Of these, more than 33,000 died. After the war, the future of African-Americans in the U.S. Army was in doubt. In July 1866, however, Congress passed legislation establishing two cavalry and four infantry regiments (later consolidated into two) whose enlisted composition was to be made up of African-Americans.

The majority of the new recruits had served in all-Black units during the war. The mounted regiments were the 9th and 10th Cavalries, soon nicknamed Buffalo Soldiers by the Cheyenne and Comanche. Until the early 1890s, they constituted 20 percent of all cavalry forces on the American frontier.*

* William Barrow, "The Buffalo Soldiers: The Negro Cavalry in the West, 1866–1891," *Black World* XVI (July 1967).

**INGREDIENTS**

½ cup flour

1 tablespoon garlic powder

1 teaspoon kosher salt

1 teaspoon black pepper, preferably freshly ground

2 pounds buffalo chuck, cut into cubes (beef may be substituted)

¼ cup canola oil

3 cups chopped onion

4 cups diced potatoes

3 cups sliced carrots

1½ cups sliced celery

Three 10½-ounce cans beef broth

1. Mix together the flour, garlic powder, salt, and pepper in a resealable plastic bag. Add the buffalo chuck, a small handful at a time, to the flour mixture and shake until well coated. Heat the oil in a large pot over high heat for 1 minute. Brown the meat, about 1 minute per side, then remove from the pot and set aside.

2. Reduce the heat to medium and sauté the onion for about 2 minutes. Add the remaining ingredients, reduce the heat to low, cover, and cook for 2 hours, stirring occasionally.

Serves 8

Note: For a thicker broth, 30 minutes before the stew is done, combine about 3 tablespoons flour and 3 tablespoons water in a small bowl. Mix well, then slowly stir into the stew.

# Robert Mays
# Lamb Da-Ra-Ja

## INGREDIENTS

1 leg of lamb or lamb ribs (3 pounds)

Salt and black pepper

12 garlic cloves

Barbecue sauce (your favorite kind!)

"I was a cook for the Santa Fe Railroad. Back then, there were four cooks on a moving train. Even as late as 1975, everything was prepared from scratch and made to order on wood-burning stoves.

"I learned a lot about cooking and choosing your meats and vegetables from my dad. Dad was a waiter on the railroad dining car, and he worked at Chicago's Stockyard Inn. He required that all his children learn how to cook.

"During family gatherings we played waitstaff, taking orders and collecting tips from unsuspecting yet appreciative relatives! When the holidays come around, we still gather at a sister's house, finding ourselves in the kitchen, making sure that everything comes together.

"I've been cooking with my younger brothers, Rick and Julius, at Real Men Cook for a few years. You can't touch the bond that these men have for one another, brothers. This event has a purpose and a goal. You reach out to the community and to those brothers, because they need to know that someone cares.

"I named this recipe after my wife, son, and daughter—Deb, Rashid, and Janeen."

1. Wash the lamb and pat dry with paper towels. Rub with salt and pepper to taste. Cut four slots in the leg or meat of the ribs and insert the garlic cloves. Put the lamb in a resealable plastic bag and refrigerate overnight.

2. Preheat the grill to medium and put the lamb over the coals. Place a drip pan under the grill so that the meat doesn't burn. Let the lamb cook slowly, for approximately 4 hours. Before serving, put barbecue sauce over the lamb.

Serves 8

**Robert Mays enjoys cooking regularly with his brother Rick at the Chicago Rib House restaurant, co-owned by family member Harry Mays.**

## Eugene Sawyer, Roderick Sawyer, Shedrick Sawyer
# The Sawyers' Red Beans and Rice—Three Ways

Mayor Sawyer (*third from left*) surrounded by his children, grandchildren, and wife at his seventieth birthday party.
PHOTO: JEROME SIMMONS PHOTOGRAPHY

### INGREDIENTS

2 pounds dried red beans (kidney beans), sorted, dirt removed, and rinsed

1 tablespoon dried thyme

One 16-ounce can stewed tomatoes, or three large tomatoes, diced

1 cup diced celery

1 cup diced yellow bell pepper

1 cup diced green bell pepper

2 bay leaves

2 pounds turkey sausage links, cut into 1-inch pieces

2 pounds medium shrimp, cleaned and deveined

"My father, former Chicago mayor Eugene Sawyer, was the greatest influence on us as far as learning how to cook, because, as he states, he had to teach my mother how to cook! The Sawyers have lived close as a family, with various groups occupying all the apartments in three- and four-unit buildings. With my grandmother close by, my sisters were in the kitchen learning with her, and I'd get up early in the morning so I could learn a few things too. That early knowledge came in handy, because at breakfast my daughter starts asking what's for dinner.

"My brother, Shedrick, who works with me, my dad, and I enjoy cooking red beans and rice. We each add our own spin to this dish, injecting a little culinary license.

"Participating with Real Men Cook celebrates the achievements of African American men—who we are, what we do. It is incumbent upon us to pave the way for the next generation."

Place the beans and thyme in a large pot and add water to cover. Cook the beans over medium heat for 1 hour. Add the remaining ingredients except the shrimp and continue to cook for 1 hour longer. Add the shrimp and cook another 20 minutes.

Serves 10 to 12

Note: You can add some gumbo filé to taste. This is excellent with okra served on the side. Filé powder is made from ground, dried leaves of the sassafras tree. To make it three ways, my brother likes it with sausage, and my dad likes it with ham hocks. Or you can fix it with just shrimp. It's all good.

**I've known the Sawyer sons most of their lives. They have followed in their father's footsteps of being strong, intelligent men who care about their family and community.—K.K.M.**

## Ron Miller

# Ron's Chicago-Style Ribs: Ribs So Good, You Don't Need Sauce

Ron Miller and his son, Brandon Miller

"I was drafted by my wife, Pepper, and good friend Marty Worrel to get involved in Real Men Cook. They knew I would feel strongly about the ideals of the event. And to be perfectly honest, I know they just wanted me to cook my world-famous ribs.

"For twelve consecutive years, my son, Brandon, and I worked together at Real Men Cook. He really grew up with the event. Participating with Brandon strengthened our bond during those years, and in that process, I felt a need to find my father after forty years of separation. I did find him, and we spent the last glorious year of his life together, all due to the experiences I had during this whole celebration of fatherhood with Real Men Cook. That experience and other personal changes in my life have led to real growth.

"I learned to cook out of necessity; my mother gave me most of the basics, and college life made it a real survival skill. While we were living around several colleges, one of my buddies decided to go to the Culinary Institute of America. I learned a lot from him while we roomed together. We threw parties, and people loved our "sets," especially the sisters. Over the years, I developed my special rib technique. After his graduation from the CIA, he challenged me to a rib-cooking thing. Well, you can imagine the rest of the story. At the end of the night, his dish was still on the table and my pans were clean.

"As long as I am standing, you will always find me at Real Men Cook with Ron's Chicago-Style Ribs: Ribs So Good, You Don't Need Sauce. Captain Bill Pinckney, the first African American to sail solo around the world, has eaten ribs from one end of the world to the other, and he sampled mine and said, 'They're the best I've ever tasted.' Case closed."

**INGREDIENTS**

1 pound baby spare ribs
(don't use precooked)

2 tablespoons seasoned
salt

1 teaspoon black
pepper

1 tablespoon garlic
powder

5 tablespoons vinegar
plus enough water
to make 2 cups
(a 15 percent
vinegar solution)

1. Trim any excess fat from the ribs. Season them with the seasoned salt, pepper, and garlic powder.

2. Heat the barbecue grill.

3. Place the seasoned ribs meat side down on the grill.

4. Turn the ribs every 15 to 20 minutes. Baste with the water and vinegar solution.

5. Cook until desired doneness.

## The key to great barbecue

1. A good even fire.
2. The meat should be turned every 15 to 20 minutes.
3. Most important for "Ron's Chicago-Style Ribs": baste with the vinegar and water mixture every time you turn the ribs.
4. Never put sauce on the ribs until they are completely done!

Serves 4

Note: My suggestion is to add sauce by request. About 50 percent of people prefer Ron's Chicago-Style Ribs without sauce. They're that good!

My recommendation for sauce is to use a commercial sauce of choice and season to taste. Some suggested seasonings include lemon juice, brown sugar, mustard, garlic, honey, and red pepper flakes. Use a cleaver or butcher knife to cut up the rib tips and separate slabs into serving portions; add sauce if desired. Accompanying dishes may include spaghetti, coleslaw, potato salad, corn on the cob, salad, and baked beans.

**Ron Miller lives in Chicago. He is a real estate broker, married, and a father.**

# Stephen Leander Carter, Sr.

# Captain Leander Carter's Famous Chesapeake Bay Fish Chowder

Stephen L. Carter, Sr.,
aka Silver—Chicago's Storyteller

"Ever since I was little, skinny, and black, my daddy, Jimmy Jones Carter, regaled my younger brother, Michael, and me with stories about his boyhood in Bushwood, Maryland—a fishing community in St. Mary's County, located on the southern portion of the Chesapeake Bay. I thought Daddy quite ingenious and nimble of toe because of the tales he related as to how he captured the famous Chesapeake Bay blue crabs using his big toe as bait.

"Equally fascinating were the stories about my grandfather, Captain Leander Carter, whose name I bear. Early in life, as history became both a school lesson and a lesson in family legacies, I was made aware that at the time of the 1860 census taken in St. Mary's County, both my grandfather—who was two at the time—and his father, William Carter, were born free men. Grandfather Leander Carter, an oysterman, dredged crabs, clams, and oysters from the Bay and ran them to markets from Baltimore to Washington, D.C., in a boat he owned called a skipjack. Granddaddy Leander was a cook on a skipjack before he bought his very own skipjack and became famous for his 'He Chowder.' The tradition of the He Chowder is that it is prepared with double the clams and double the fish.

"In 1978 I bought a copy of historical novelist James A. Michener's *Chesapeake*. Michener's literary fame was matched by his reputation for the extensive research he did on the locale of his novels. Partway through the book I became fascinated by a character named Cudjo, a captured African of the Yoruba nation, who led a successful slave ship uprising aboard the fictional ship *Bristol*.

"In the course of the story, Cudjo gains his freedom in America and adopts the surname of a former antagonist, Cater. I initially gave little thought to the similarity of the fictional character's name and mine (Cater/Carter). But further into the novel, I was struck silent by some lines: Cudjo Cater's son, Jimbo, scuffles, saves, and buys a skipjack—a substantial investment of capital for that time. Jimbo, as he walks away from his 9-to-5, so to speak, tells his former boss, 'My Daddy tol' me,

1 cup chopped celery

½ cup diced onion

2 tablespoons butter

1¼ cups diced new red potatoes

1 tablespoon black pepper, preferably freshly ground

1 tablespoon cayenne pepper

1 tablespoon Hungarian paprika

1 tablespoon kosher or seasoned salt

1 cup heavy cream (half-and-half or milk may be substituted)

1½ cups shredded sharp Cheddar cheese

1 pound monkfish fillet, cut into cubes (halibut may be substituted)

2 dozen washed cherrystone clams (littlenecks may be substituted)

4 green onions, green parts only, chopped, for garnish

"Git yourself a boat! When a man got his own boat—he free. His onliest prison—the horizon." '

"I don't know for certain if Michener used my grandfather as inspiration for his character. Nevertheless, I feel in my heart that my grandfather, Captain Leander Carter, and my daddy, Jimmy Jones Carter, embody the same spirit of freedom as Cudjo and Jimbo Cater. I am proud to realize that we, as African American men, have a rich culinary and entrepreneurial heritage."

1. Sauté the celery and onion in the butter.

2. Place 4 quarts water into a 6- to 8-quart seasoned cast-iron pot (Dutch oven). Add the potatoes, black pepper, cayenne, paprika, salt, celery, and onion. Bring to a slow boil over medium-low heat and cook for 40 minutes. Let cool slightly, then add the heavy cream slowly so that it doesn't curdle. Gradually add the cheese, stirring frequently. Bring to a slow boil, then simmer over low heat for about 10 minutes, stirring frequently.

3. Add the fish and clams and cook for 5 minutes. Pour the chowder into a serving bowl and garnish with the green onions. Serve with French or Italian bread.

Serves 6 to 8

**Stephen Leander Carter, Sr., aka Silver—Chicago's Storyteller, is the proud son of Jimmy Jones Carter, proud grandson of Captain Leander Carter, and proud legacy bearer of Cudjo and Jimbo Cater.**

# William Higgonbotham
# Red Velvet Cake

William Higgonbotham

**INGREDIENTS**

½ cup vegetable shortening

1½ cups sugar

2 eggs

One or two 1-ounce bottles red food coloring

2 tablespoons vanilla extract

2½ cups sifted flour

½ teaspoon salt

2 teaspoons unsweetened cocoa powder

1 cup buttermilk

1 tablespoon white vinegar

1 teaspoon baking soda

Cream Cheese Frosting (below)

Chopped pecans, for garnish

"I grew up during the Depression, and we didn't have a lot of things in the house that most kids had. So we helped the grown-ups whenever we could.

"I had my first economics lesson when I was very young. I'd sell cupcakes out of our kitchen window, and one day my grandmother asked me how much I was selling them for. I thought I was really on target—and on the money—selling those cupcakes for two or three cents apiece. When I told her that, my feelings got a little hurt because I didn't realize that we were losing money because every cupcake had to pay for the butter, sugar, and flour that went into it.

"Back then, all the men in my family had to learn how to cook, sew, and iron—in the event your wife wasn't feeling up to it, you could help out . . . or if you stayed single, you could help yourself.

"I have always enjoyed sweets and pastries, so the Red Velvet Cake is a good old southern dessert to prepare.

"My son-in-law, Mel Monroe, brought me into Real Men Cook to help him out. Once we got started and saw the admiration, the happiness, the togetherness, it became one thing after another. I thought it just ignites something in you that you want to be a part of . . . and I'm glad I was."

1. Preheat the oven to 350°F. Grease and flour three 8-inch cake pans.

2. Beat the vegetable shortening at medium speed with an electric mixer until fluffy. Gradually add the sugar and continue to beat well. Add the eggs one at a time, beating after each addition until blended. Stir in the food coloring and vanilla and blend well.

3. Combine the flour, salt, and cocoa and set aside. Combine the buttermilk, vinegar, and baking soda in a 4-cup liquid measuring cup: the mixture will bubble. Add the flour mixture to the shortening mixture, alternating with the buttermilk mixture, beginning and ending with the flour mixture. Beat at low speed after each addition until blended. Beat at medium speed for 2 minutes. Pour the batter into the prepared pans.

**INGREDIENTS**

One 8-ounce package cream cheese, softened

¼ pound (1 stick) butter or margarine, softened

One 1-pound box confectioners' sugar, sifted

1 teaspoon vanilla extract

Bake for 25 minutes. Allow the layers to cool completely on wire racks before frosting. Spread the frosting between the layers and on top of the cake, then garnish with chopped pecans.

Serves 8

## Cream Cheese Frosting

Beat the cream cheese and butter until fluffy. Gradually add the confectioners' sugar, beating at low speed until blended. Add the vanilla, beating until well blended.

Makes about 3½ cups (enough for a 3-layer cake)

**William Higgonbotham passed away on February 15, 2001. His energy and love for his family speaks to what Real Men are made of, strength and dedication.—K.K.M.**

## Mel Monroe
# Po' Folk Sea Summer Salad

Mel Monroe

"I didn't grow up with a father, and my-father-in-law, William Higgonbotham, was like a father to me. He set an example for me and paved the way for me to be the man that I am."

1. Cook the noodles according to package directions, adding the margarine and a pinch of salt to the water—do not overcook. Drain, cool, and season to taste with garlic powder and onion powder. Add 3 tablespoons of the olive oil, and stir to combine. Add the crabmeat and undrained minced clams. Mix well.

2. Cook the shrimp for 1 minute over medium heat in a nonstick skillet. Cool and slice each shrimp in half lengthwise. Add the salt, pepper, and 2 teaspoons of the olive oil. Add the shrimp to the noodle mixture and gently combine.

## INGREDIENTS

2 pounds spiral rotini noodles (elbows or another shape pasta may be substituted)

1 tablespoon margarine

Pinch of salt

Garlic powder

Onion powder

6 tablespoons plus 2 teaspoons olive oil

½ pound imitation crabmeat

Two 6-ounce cans minced clams, with juice

½ pound medium shrimp, peeled and deveined

1 teaspoon salt

1 teaspoon black pepper

1 garlic clove, sliced

1 cup chopped red onion

1 cup chopped green bell pepper *(Use red or yellow peppers if they're on sale.)*

One 8-ounce jar olives *(Use black or assorted Spanish olives, pitted*

¼ cup chopped celery *(Use hearts of palm if you got paid this week.)*

1 cup balsamic vinegar *(Use whatever brand that's on sale.)*

3 tablespoons wine *(Use whatever kind you've got!)*

2 tablespoons sugar

½ pound feta cheese, crumbled *(Use the cheapest.)*

¼ pound chopped nuts *(Use walnuts, pecans, pine nuts, or whatever is on sale.)*

3. In a separate bowl, combine the garlic, onion, green pepper, olives, and celery. Add the vinegar, the remaining 3 tablespoons olive oil, and the wine. Add the sugar slowly, stirring until dissolved. Add to the noodle mixture and combine gently. Garnish with the feta cheese and nuts. Cover and chill for 2 to 3 hours. Stir again before serving.

Serves 8

Note: For extra spice, add ¼ cup gardenaria mix just before adding the feta cheese. For best results, serve over a bed of romaine lettuce.

## CHAPTER TWO

# The Biggest Room in the House

The kitchen is the "biggest room in the house" for many reasons. It is the room where we talk, share, gather, laugh, and cry. It's a haven.

My maternal grandmother worked for some of the wealthiest families in Cleveland, Ohio. When the schedule required special attention due to large dinner parties and other such functions, she would stay over in quarters provided for her use. Oftentimes, these quarters were replete with her own personal kitchen area in addition to a bath and bedroom. Many times, when I would visit Cleveland from Chicago, I'd spend the night in the quarters with her.

To my young eyes, these houses looked like castles. The large, numerous rooms provided hours of enchantment for my imagination. Fueled by the radio adventure serials and suspense films of the day, I imagined hidden passageways behind the walls and eyes following my every move from behind paintings of people long dead. I was convinced the portraits covered wall safes chock-full of money and jewels.

However charmed I was by these environments, I spent most of my time in the kitchen, which had wonders of its own to behold. There were walk-in food lockers, wine closets, and custom-built refrigerators with multiple doors. Inside these treasure chests was an endless array of foods that were not common at home. Much of our family's notion of exotic fruits and vegetables and expensive cuts of meat, fish, and fowl, as well as the condiments and garnishes to properly serve an elegant meal, came as a result of this kind of exposure. From these experiences, both my mother and I learned the value and care of fine china, glassware, and silverware. Under my grandmother's direction, professional chefs, assistants, and other extra staff who knew how to make full use of such great kitchen facilities labored diligently to produce events of epic proportion. It was like sitting in a classroom as I looked on from some secure corner lest I get caught underfoot.

The kitchen we had at home in Chicago was not as fancy, but it was equally dedicated to the production of tasty fare. After a day of Saturday shopping, my father and I were sufficiently hungry so that a snack was in order to hold us over until dinner was ready. Crackers and cheese (Swiss, Cheddar, and American) sufficed for me. Sometimes I'd have an egg sandwich. My father was a lover of Limburger—the putrid-smelling "stinky cheese." It had to be wrapped in cheesecloth, covered with waxed paper, and kept in a jar that was sealed with a rubber ring to keep it from contaminating other things in the fridge. At any rate, he ate his cheese served with a slice of onion, pickles, or olives, and a tall, ice-cold glass of beer. I drank milk, preferably chocolate.

Meanwhile, a heavy iron pot braised shanks of lamb that had

been dusted with flour so they'd brown on all sides, then sprinkled with salt, pepper (black and red), olive oil, and a little water. The lid was kept on. Open it up and check, adding carrots, a little celery, fresh green and red sweet peppers, onions, garlic, new potatoes. Turn again, add some red wine (Momma's best, if not too sweet that year), lower the flame, and wait . . . and wait . . . It would be hours before simmer became supper.

These recipes reflect family gatherings. Family meals, casseroles, big pots of chili on the stove. For Terry Allen, his Funeral Grieving Brand Cake tells the story of how this cake was given to a grieving family. Sporty King's Macaroni and Cheeze—with a *z*— is a dish that is a tradition during the holidays and southern tradition for Sunday supper. And what would a family gathering be without John Russell's Apple Peach Cobbler? You will find that these recipes, as do most of them throughout this book, evoke fond memories of family gatherings and traditions that have been passed down from generation to generation.

## Darryl Dennard
# Darryl's Dynamite Chicken Wings

Darryl Dennard

**INGREDIENTS**

2 to 3 pounds chicken wings, cut in half, wing tips discarded

Salt and black pepper

Paprika

2 cups vegetable oil

DYNAMITE SAUCE:

½ cup Louisiana hot sauce

1 tablespoon butter or margarine

1 tablespoon white distilled vinegar

1 teaspoon sugar

Juice of ½ orange

"Growing up in New York, I had a father who was somewhat eclectic. I was exposed to a variety of ethnic foods and shown how to shop for and prepare many types of foods. As a result, I now shop all over Chicago to find whatever I might be seeking for a real flavorful experience and an authentic taste.

"My mother and grandmother prepared me early in life for living on my own. When I was seventeen, I left home for college. While in school, I roomed with some buddies off campus and all of us practiced our cooking skills, and if I do say so myself, we did pretty well.

"I am still a pretty good cook. Chicken is a specialty of mine: stir-fried, Hawaiian, cacciatore, scaloppine, or Buffalo wings. You name it, I can cook it.

"As one of the original cooks in Real Men Cook, I remember that first event. There was a great crew of people who believed in the vision of Real Men Cook, and it gave us an opportunity to come together and showcase some talented people."

1. Season the wings with salt, pepper, and paprika to taste. Fry in hot oil over medium heat for 5 to 7 minutes, then remove and drain.

2. Combine all of the Dynamite Sauce ingredients in a small saucepan and simmer over a low flame until the sugar is dissolved.

3. Place the wings in a pot and pour the sauce over them. Cover the pot and shake until the sauce coats the wings. Serve while hot with store-bought blue cheese dressing and celery and carrot sticks.

Serves 6 to 8

**Darryl Dennard is the director of communications at Kennedy-King College, one of the City Colleges of Chicago and host of the nationally syndicated _Minority Business Report._**

Howard Hill

# Howard's International Turkey Chili

## INGREDIENTS

2 pounds ground turkey

Three 28-ounce cans red kidney beans (light), with liquid

Two 28-ounce cans red kidney beans (dark), with liquid

One 1¼-ounce package chili seasoning mix

Two 28-ounce cans stewed tomatoes

One 8-ounce can tomato sauce

2 large garlic cloves, chopped

2 jalapeño peppers, seeded and chopped

1 tablespoon chili powder

1 tablespoon garlic powder

1 red bell pepper, chopped

½ medium onion, chopped

½ tablespoon dried oregano

Turkey is gaining in popularity with non-red-meat eaters, and this recipe is great with or without the turkey. It includes both light and dark red kidney beans. Dried beans, or legumes, are rich in protein, calcium, phosphorus, and iron, and appear in the diet of almost every culture. Serve this dish at a Super Bowl Party with all of the trimmings. You might want to double the recipe, because there will be nothing left after your friends taste this delicious chili. Freeze the second batch for yourself.

Place the ground turkey into a skillet and brown over medium heat. Put the remaining ingredients into large stock pot and cook for 20 minutes over medium heat. Add the browned turkey and simmer for 15 minutes over low heat. Serve with sour cream, shredded Cheddar cheese, and your favorite crackers.

Serves 6 to 8

James Battiste

# James's Fried Chicken

James Battiste

**INGREDIENTS**

2 whole chickens
(3 pounds each), cut
into serving pieces

2 cups whole milk

2 large garlic cloves,
smashed

2 cups flour

2 teaspoons garlic
powder

1 teaspoon dried sage,
crumbled

1 tablespoon salt

1 teaspoon cayenne
pepper

1 teaspoon black
pepper

1 teaspoon onion
powder

1 teaspoon poultry
seasoning

1 teaspoon sugar

1 cup peanut oil

This isn't your mother's fried chicken. This recipe has a few added spices to make it a welcome addition to your dinner repertoire. Serve this with gravy over rice and mouth-watering hot biscuits. Your mother won't mind a new twist on this southern favorite.

1. Place the chicken in a large shallow bowl. Pour in the milk and garlic; cover and refrigerate overnight.

2. Combine the flour and seasonings in a pie plate and mix well. Remove the chicken from the milk and dip into the flour mixture, lightly coating all sides.

3. Heat half of the oil to about 300°F in a large heavy-bottomed skillet. Add the chicken, a few pieces at a time; do not crowd. Fry until browned and crisp, about 15 minutes per side. Drain well on a plate lined with paper towels. Add more oil as necessary and fry the remaining chicken.

Serves 6 to 8

John Russell

# Apple Peach Cobbler

INGREDIENTS

4 pounds apples,
peeled and cored

4 pounds peaches

1 pound (4 sticks)
butter, melted

4 cups light corn syrup

4 cups flour

2 tablespoons salt

1 pound (4 sticks)
butter

Cobblers are a deep-dish fruit dessert with a biscuit-type crust and topping. They are delicious and are made with a variety of fruit mixtures.

1. Preheat the oven to 350°F.

2. Cut the apples and peaches into pieces. Combine the melted butter and syrup and add the fruit to the mixture; set aside.

3. Combine the flour, salt, and butter and mix well; press about three-quarters of the crust into the bottom of a large roaster pan. Pour the fruit mixture over the crust and sprinkle with the remaining crust mixture. Bake for about 45 minutes or until golden brown.

Serves 12 to 14

## Joseph C. Phillips

# Nic's Roasted Garlic Soup

**INGREDIENTS**

2 large garlic bulbs

1 large shallot bulb

3 tablespoons olive oil

4 sprigs thyme, tied together in pairs

1 cup sliced onion

3 large garlic cloves, chopped

1 bay leaf

5 cups chicken broth

1 tablespoon chopped fresh thyme

¼ cup heavy cream

1 cup fresh bread crumbs

Salt and black pepper

Garlic has long been credited with providing strength to the Egyptians. For many centuries, its medicinal properties were claimed to cure toothaches, open wounds, and, well, even spirits. It is a member of the lily family and is a cousin to leeks, chives, onions, and shallots. Crushing, chopping, or pureeing garlic releases more oils and will give a sharper taste than sliced garlic. Roasted garlic, which is baked unpeeled garlic, is very sweet.

This soup is marvelous with fish or shrimp stock substituted for the chicken, and you can garnish it with chopped shrimp, bay scallops, or rock shrimp.

1. Preheat the oven to 400°F.

2. Place the garlic and shallot bulbs on two separate squares of aluminum foil. Drizzle with 1 tablespoon of the olive oil, put the thyme sprigs on top, and wrap foil loosely around bulbs. Roast for about 1 hour. Peel and chop the garlic and shallot after roasting.

3. Heat the remaining 2 tablespoons olive oil in a soup kettle or medium stock pot. Sauté the onion for 2 minutes, add the chopped garlic, and continue cooking until the onion is translucent. Add the roasted garlic and shallot, thyme sprigs, bay leaf, and broth. Simmer over medium-low heat for 45 minutes. Remove the thyme sprigs. Add the chopped thyme, cream, and bread crumbs.

4. When the bread is soft, and the soup has cooled slightly, puree the soup in a blender or food processor until the texture is smooth. Add salt and pepper to taste, return the soup to the stock pot, reheat, and serve.

Serves 4

Kahari Walton

# Kahari's Drunken Chicken

## INGREDIENTS

1 tablespoon chili powder

1 tablespoon paprika

½ tablespoon onion powder

½ tablespoon garlic powder

½ tablespoon ground cumin

½ tablespoon white or black pepper

1 tablespoon salt

¼ tablespoon dried basil

¼ teaspoon dried thyme

2 pounds split chicken breasts, with skin

One 18-ounce bottle barbecue sauce

½ cup light brown sugar

1 tablespoon crushed red pepper flakes

¾ cup bourbon

2 bay leaves

Kahari's father, Chaga Walton, has been my right hand, ambassador, and "savior" on many fronts. Kahari is a proud, strong, and mature young man who, like his father, is always ready to extend his hand and his heart to Real Men Cook and the community.

1. Preheat the grill. Combine the chili powder, paprika, onion powder, garlic powder, cumin, pepper, salt, basil, and thyme to make the rub. Wash the chicken and pat dry with paper towels, then put on a flat surface and season with the rub.

2. Pour the barbecue sauce into a pot and turn the heat to medium. Fill the empty bottle about a quarter of the way with water. Swish the water around and add to the pot with the barbecue sauce. Add the brown sugar, red pepper flakes, bourbon, and bay leaves. Reduce the heat to low and simmer for about 15 to 20 minutes, stirring occasionally.

3. Place the chicken on the grill and cook until done, brushing the sauce on at the end of the grilling process. Remove the chicken from the grill and brush on sauce, completely covering the chicken. Let cool and enjoy!

Serves 4

# Ken Brown

# World-Famous Broccoli Chicken

Ken Brown

**INGREDIENTS**

¼ cup vegetable oil

5 pounds boneless, skinless chicken breasts, cut into 1-inch pieces

8 cups broccoli florets

1 cup chicken broth

1 tablespoon Old Bay seasoning

1¼ cups oyster sauce

1¼ cups soy sauce

5 cups cooked rice

"Cooking is special for me because it's the art of making people happy.

"I get a lot of my inspiration from my grandmother; she is Creole from New Orleans. She is the best cook in town. I would always say, 'Granny, you're getting older, you've got to write down that recipe.' Her response, like most ladies of that era, was, 'I don't have a recipe.' She would take a pinch of this and that . . . and to this day she's still like that.

"My father, who was a chef and restaurateur in Tampa, made me want to cook professionally, but to be honest, the memory of my grandmother's home cooking is what drives me to wake up on Saturday morning and prepare either a big killer breakfast or a big dinner.

"Why do I participate in Real Men Cook? Because the people who come there remember you from past years and remember your dish, and to have someone come up to you and say, 'You know, I've been waiting all year for this dish'—man, you can't put a price tag on that.

"One year, my dad—who had promised me for several years that he would come—was supposed to be my guest, and as you would have it, we were shoulder to shoulder and he was helping me cook."

Heat a wok or large sauté pan until it is very hot. Add the oil and heat for 30 seconds. Add the chicken and cook until golden brown. Add the broccoli and broth and cook for about 4 minutes. Add the Old Bay seasoning, oyster sauce, and soy sauce, and stir-fry away. Serve over rice.

Serves 12 to 14

Note: If you like, garnish with a few julienne strips of red and green bell pepper for color.

**Ken Brown was the coordinator for the 2004 Real Men Cook in Detroit. His magnetism and love for people shows, as his booth always draws a crowd.—K.K.M.**

## Ken McKay
# Ken's Strawberry Pie

**INGREDIENTS**

1 tablespoon
confectioners' sugar

1 cup plus 1 tablespoon
milk

One 8-ounce package
cream cheese

1 package instant
lemon pie filling

One 9-inch graham
cracker piecrust

One 10-ounce bag
frozen strawberries

One 8-ounce container
Cool Whip

"My roots are from Mississippi on my mother's side and Tennessee on my father's side. There is a history of men in my family who cook, but generally the women did all of the cooking. Yet the men always had a specialty here and there, and they would stick by it very strongly. My father, especially—he could make some mean salmon croquettes. You just couldn't touch it. And he made some good smothered potatoes; nobody wanted to touch that. So there were some dishes that my father stood by real strongly, and I'd stand by them with him.

"I enjoy good food and good cooking. I had always wanted to be a part of Real Men Cook. The idea of men getting out and doing something positive is something that attracts my consciousness. The Father's Day celebration exemplifies the kind of leadership we do have in our community, and it's an opportunity to be front and center onstage. Real Men Cook is not about competition. It is about how we can complement one another, but of course there's always bragging rights, and we encourage that. I am a cooking man and I love to be around brothers who like to show off their stuff—their masterpieces from the oven or the grill. Recruiting the men, getting the brothers to volunteer, and motivating them helps me to reinforce the importance of the bonding and friendship with the other guys. I certainly expected it to be a festive occasion, and I'm one of those people who really likes to be around good people having good fun. It's the fellowship and camaraderie with other men that makes Real Men Cook more than just a gathering—it's a brotherhood. Especially since my father passed, the event has great sentimental value to me."

1. Combine the sugar, 1 tablespoon milk, and the cream cheese with an electric mixer until you get a smooth consistency.

2. In a separate bowl, mix the lemon pie filling with 1 cup milk until smooth.

3. Layer the ingredients as follows in the graham cracker crust: first the cream cheese mixture, then the strawberries, then the lemon filling, and top with the Cool Whip. For best results, refrigerate overnight. Enjoy!

Serves 6 to 8

# Lorenzo E. Martin

# Sour Cream Gingerbread

Lorenzo E. Martin

### INGREDIENTS

¼ pound (1 stick) butter

1 cup granulated sugar

½ cup molasses

½ cup sour cream

2 eggs

1½ cups flour

1 teaspoon baking powder

½ teaspoon salt

½ teaspoon ground ginger

¼ cup confectioners' sugar (optional)

Lorenzo E. Martin lived next door to me from when I was six years old until I went to college. I practically lived in the Martin house. His grandmother, Mrs. House, baked bread every single day. We didn't know what store-bought bread was. As kids we wanted to taste that Wonder bread. We had no appreciation that we were privileged to enjoy the real deal, home-baked bread, every day. Between Lorenzo's grandmother and his mother, there was always a lot of baking going on. The aroma of freshly baked loaves of bread and hot rolls poured through the neighborhood. Baking was serious business in the Martin household. Mr. Martin, a Pullman porter, cooked too. During the summertime, I can remember him and my dad, Arnold Saunders, sitting around the card table with family and friends. What fond memories . . .

1. Preheat the oven to 350°F. Butter and lightly flour a 9-inch square pan.

2. Cream the butter and slowly add the sugar, beating until light and fluffy. Add the molasses and sour cream and blend well. Add the eggs, continuing to beat until well mixed. Add the flour, baking powder, salt, and ginger and beat until smooth. Pour the batter into the prepared pan and bake for 30 to 40 minutes, until a toothpick inserted into the center of the cake comes out clean. Let cool for 10 minutes, then dust with the confectioners' sugar if desired.

Serves 6 to 8

**Lorenzo E. Martin is the publisher of the *Chicago Standard Newspaper* and the *Chicago South Suburban Standard.***

Otis Henderson

# This Ain't Momma's Tuna Casserole

### INGREDIENTS

1 pound tri-color pasta (any shape)

1 cup sliced carrots

One 10¾-ounce can condensed cream of celery soup

1 cup half-and-half

1½ cups grated Cheddar cheese (about ¾ pound)

½ cup sliced celery

2 cups chopped broccoli florets

1 cup diced onion

Two 6-ounce cans solid white tuna in oil, drained

One 10-ounce package frozen baby peas

Everyone's grandmother and mother have their own versions of this classic, quick, one-dish meal. It's made with ingredients you should always have on hand for that last-minute meal you can cook up in a flash. It isn't Momma's, it's better!

1. Preheat the oven to 350°F.

2. Cook the pasta and carrots in boiling water for 5 minutes, drain, and set aside.

3. Combine the soup and half-and-half and heat slowly. Add the cheese to the mixture, stirring slowly until the cheese is melted.

4. In a large mixing bowl, combine the celery, broccoli, onion, tuna, peas, carrots, and pasta. Add the cheese sauce and mix thoroughly. Pour into a 2- or 2½-quart casserole dish and bake for 20 minutes.

Serves 6

## Sporty King
# Macaroni and Cheeze

Sporty King

### INGREDIENTS

1 pound elbow
macaroni

½ pound sharp
Cheddar cheese

½ pound mild Cheddar
cheese

¾ pound American
cheese

¼ pound (1 stick) butter
or margarine, melted

2 eggs, beaten

¾ cup diced onion

½ cup milk

¼ teaspoon black
pepper

½ teaspoon Lawry's
seasoned salt

Paprika

"I enjoy cooking because I enjoy eating. My favorite dish is macaroni and cheeze (with a z), using the government cheese. When I was in corporate America—at *The Wall Street Journal*—I ate out a lot. But now as a professional speaker, I'm on my own schedule.

"Along with cooking, one of my other passions is youth development. Anything that I can do to help these kids develop and grow, I do it. I've done a lot of refereeing and coaching basketball. The fact that Real Men Cook benefits some youth organizations appeals to me. If we're serious about helping children develop, we also have to help adults develop. It doesn't do a kid any good today to have a good experience with somebody on the outside and then when they go home, they have to face a bad experience with their families. Real Men Cook gives all of the men the opportunity to help these young kids—our future leaders—to develop into *Real Men*. I hear it all the time: this Father's Day celebration brings a lot of men closer to their families. And for everyone, it's like a big family reunion."

1. Preheat the oven to 350°F.

2. Cook the macaroni according to package directions. Cut the cheese into small squares or chunks and place in an 8 by 8-inch baking dish. When the macaroni is done, drain, but save a little of the cooking water. Pour the macaroni and reserved water on top of the cheese. Stir slightly so that the cheese can melt evenly. This will give each noodle a "cheesy" taste, and you won't have any uncoated macaroni.

3. Combine the butter, eggs, onion, milk, pepper, and seasoned salt. Mix together and pour over the macaroni. Stir again to distribute the cheese. Generously shake paprika over the dish. Bake for about 30 minutes.

Serves 4 to 6

**Sporty King is a professional speaker in Chicago.**

Steve Bluford

# Roasted Ribeye Steak

## INGREDIENTS

¾ cup tequila

2 tablespoons orange juice

2 tablespoons minced garlic

1 tablespoon minced onion

1 tablespoon McCormick Grill Mates Montreal Steak Marinade

1 tablespoon light brown sugar

2 ribeye steaks (½ pound each)

"My father was a professor, but he was also a cook, and he was the one who taught me how to cook. Cooking is one of my hobbies; I enjoy it and I love to see other people eat. It's a great feeling when someone comes up to you and says, 'Hey, man, I really enjoyed your dish.'

"When I was about ten or eleven, I would hang around and watch my father throw down on the grill. A little bit of this and a pinch of that, and he'd always come up to me and grab me and say, 'Taste this!' Cooking was the world to him, and he passed that on to me. Growing up, I was always in the kitchen. I could have been out playing ball with the other kids, but my mother would always remind us that if she wasn't home, and if we wanted to eat, we would have to cook.

"I love to try different foods. You have to keep your mind and taste buds open to new things. I'm always trying something new with my cooking. My wife does most of the shopping, but I buy all of the herbs and spices. I'm a little deeper into discovering flavor. It's the seasoning that makes all the difference in the food. No matter what you're fixing, it makes a world of difference. If it ain't properly seasoned, ain't no need in even cooking it.

"Real Men Cook allows me to do two things that I care about most: I like to give something to the public and share good food. *Period!*"

1. In a shallow, nonreactive dish, combine all of the marinade ingredients. Reserve ½ cup marinade for basting. Place the steaks in the mixture. Cover and marinate for 1 hour in the refrigerator.

2. Preheat an outdoor grill for high heat, and lightly oil the grate. Grill the steaks for 5 to 7 minutes per side, to desired doneness. Use the reserved marinade to baste the steaks while grilling. Discard any remaining marinade. (You may also cook the steaks in the oven: Preheat the oven to 375°F. Place the marinated steaks in a lightly buttered casserole dish. Roast for 10 minutes, or until desired doneness.)

Serves 2

# Terry Allen
## Funeral Grieving Brand Cake

Terry Allen

"Since 1907, my family compound in Plano, Texas, has been the site of annual cookouts and gatherings where great-grands and grandfathers prepared meats from the smokehouse in the back of the house. We have had two family restaurants. My uncle, who specialized in desserts, played an important part in my early years of learning how to cook. My grandmother has, in a cedar chest, a copy of a cookbook with all of the family recipes that have been passed down. This is a written history, preserved·for the next generation. These recipes have been built around our lives.

"I'm the oldest of twelve children, and many of us still gather at our grandmother's house. The movie *Soul Food* is a page out of our family's life. We all cook and talk about the challenges at work and what's going on with the children. Most of my brothers and sisters have two or three children. It's a full house, filled with a lot of love and laughter.

"Funerals in Texas and in my family were the only times somber met with celebration. We all came from or lived in segregated communities back in the day. One plus of the 'old dirty South' was, while segregated, the community showed its peacock colors when someone was born, a house was built or purchased, and when someone died. Death was a ritual-based event in my family. Pictures were swapped; wills were read; long-parted friends and family were reunited. In the midst of it all, an ancient African tradition of caring for the survivors of the deceased through food, money, housing, and clothing was there! Since we all were descendants of enslaved Africans and/or Native Americans, the quest to be seen as equal was high for the residents in our communities. That being so, during visitation and funeralization, we dressed to the nines, wearing outfits that may have taken a week's wages to buy. The simple act of feeding the bereaved would become a task fit for a king's coronation. A feast of food was prepared and sent to the homes of the affected families. Funny, though—the grieving parties never ate much, but everyone else did! Visitors stuffed themselves well. So it was important that the bereaved, who ate less than anyone, got energy and sustenance, so the sugar-laden, fat-filled funeral cake and peach cobbler filled the need.

6 Sunny Meadow
brown eggs

¾ pound (3 sticks) Land
O Lakes home-style
butter

One 8-ounce package
Philadelphia cream
cheese

3 cups Imperial pure
cane sugar

1 Texas (piled high)
tablespoon Arm &
Hammer baking soda

1 Texas teaspoon
Calumet baking
powder straight out of
the red tin

3 cups Gold Medal
unbleached flour

¾ cup (a Lubbock,
Texas, coffee mug–size
cup) Borden's
sweetened condensed
milk

1 teaspoon Adam's
vanilla extract

1 teaspoon Crisco

It gave the bereaved in my family a temporary holdover till their appetites returned. Now, you will see in the funeral cake recipe that the brands were important, because if you did not use the right name brands, you might as well be buried right along with the deceased."

1. Beat those eggs throughly in a small bowl with a strong arm, making a nice blend.

2. Melt the butter all day, or as long as it takes to melt. Blend the butter, cream cheese, and sugar together. Now add the eggs, making a mixture.

3. Use a sifter to sift the baking soda, baking powder, and flour unto a large red clay mixing bowl. Add about half of the dry ingredients to the butter mixture and take that Texas arm and a large mixing spoon and stir that bowl up real good. Pour in the milk, mix it, then add the remaining flour mixture. After blending, add the vanilla.

4. Take your finger and spread the Crisco very, very lightly on the insides of three 7 by 7-inch metal cake pans. Bake in the stone oven about three or four logs hot (that is 350°F for you urban professionals). Bake until they have all risen nice and brown (again, for you urbanites, 30 to 35 minutes). Let cool on waxed paper. Now get that chocolate icing recipe and frost the cake. The grieving parties who are not eating well or much can survive a day or two on a few slices of this energy-driven cake.

Serves 6 to 8

**Terry Allen is a single father with one son. He is a public relations and marketing consultant at Southern Methodist University.**

The Dudleys (Del-Re Dudley; Carlton Dudley, Sr.; and Carlton Dudley, Jr.)

# Charlene's Succulent Salmon Loaf

"I was exposed to the art of cooking very early in my life," says Del-Re Dudley. "My dad, Carlton Sr., was a chef, trained at the Washburne Culinary Institute, in Chicago, and my maternal grandfather was a butcher. My grandparents had a farm, and they used to tell me about 'working the fields' and being raised with crowder peas, greens, corn, and staple vegetables. My grandfather would hunt and fish and cook the daily catch right on the river. And at one point in time, I owned a seafood store, keeping up the family tradition of being in the food industry.

"Cooking is special to me because it sparks my creativity. I like taking a recipe and putting it together, adding my own little twists and nuances to it. Putting my own signature to it really excites me.

"I can eat Japanese, Indian, French, and Italian—variety is a key spice to life. I consider myself a gourmet in training, yet I always remind myself that you're never going to be as good as you want to be, but you're always striving for perfection.

"For me Real Men Cook is a family event. I recruited my dad one year, then my brother, Carlton Jr. After that it became a standing drill. I like mixing it up and trying something new every year, keeping it fresh and exciting."

"We do Real Men Cook as a family of men," says Carlton D. Dudley, father of Del-Re and Carlton Jr. "For me it's therapeutic, the volunteering. I do a lot of volunteer work. I'm a recovering alcoholic, so I lecture. I'd say over a period of time I've talked to thousands of people in jails, mental institutions, and hospitals about the drinking and drug thing. That's also a way of keeping that problem of mine up front, and they say volunteers live longer. The people who don't volunteer on earth are going to have to do a lot of it in the afterlife—at a very high temperature!"

Two 14-ounce cans
pink salmon

2 cups shredded
mozzarella cheese

½ cup grated Parmesan
cheese

2 eggs plus 2 egg whites

¼ cup finely chopped
green onions (green
and white parts)

3 tablespoons flour

2 tablespoons butter

1 cup milk

Black pepper to taste

½ cup Béarnaise Sauce

(below)

¾ cup bread crumbs

CRUST:

¼ pound cream cheese

¼ pound (1 stick) butter

1½ cups flour

¼ teaspoon salt

BEARNAISE SAUCE:

3 tablespoons flour

2 egg yolks

1. Mix the salmon and spine/bones until well combined. Add 1 cup of the mozzarella, the Parmesan, eggs and egg whites, green onions, flour, butter, milk, pepper to taste, and Béarnaise Sauce. Mix well and set aside.

2. Mix the crust ingredients together and refrigerate for 1 hour.

3. Preheat the oven to 350°F. Grease a 9 by 4 by 3-inch loaf pan and sprinkle evenly with the bread crumbs. Put in the remaining 1 cup mozzarella, then add the salmon mixture. Remove the dough from the refrigerator and shape into a rectangle in proportion to the baking pan. Place the dough in between two sheets of plastic wrap and roll out into a rectangle 1 inch larger than the size of the pan. Top with the crust. Bake for 30 minutes, or until lightly browned.

Serves 6

## Béarnaise Sauce

Combine the flour and egg yolks in a double boiler or small saucepan and cook over low heat, stirring constantly, until smooth and thick.

**Charlene is an older cousin to Del-Re Dudley. She is the family's most prominent cooking icon. She is also the gatekeeper to the Dudleys' most secret recipes.—K.K.M**

# CHAPTER THREE

# The Shy Chick from Fox Lake

In 1948 the cabin "Shy Chick" became part of my family history. That was the year my maternal grandmother, Bessie Moore, along with her second husband, who we called Uncle Walter, purchased the property at 50 Wilson Drive in Fox Lake, Indiana. Momma Bess was a domestic. Uncle Walter, who in earlier years had been a professional tap dancer, was a superintendent for the Cleveland, Ohio, Department of Sanitation.

In the late 1940s, working-class black folk were just beginning to gain a little security. If they worked hard and saved their money, it was possible for them to buy property. Momma Bess heard about Fox Lake, a small fishing lake outside the city of Angola, from the wealthy white families she worked for. They talked of a place in Indiana where "Negroes"—black doctors, lawyers, morticians, and teachers from various cities in Michigan, Ohio, and Indiana—could purchase lakefront property. My grandmother aspired to be one of those "Negroes."

The road to her very own Fox Lake cabin started when she was a young girl. My grandmother never considered herself a servant; she was a professional domestic engineer and developed a legendary reputation among the wealthiest families in Cleveland. She was able to choose "what kind of people" she would work for, and her well-heeled employers were compelled to comply with her desire to be addressed as "*Mrs.* Moore."

The house the Moores purchased at 50 Wilson Drive sat just at the top of the hill overlooking Fox Lake. It was a two-story wood-frame cabin with three bedrooms and a small living room/kitchen/family room. Its upper and lower porches were mercifully screened in from the "gallon nippers" (mosquitoes). This purchase changed Mrs. Moore's work schedule significantly. Her already generous six-week annual hiatus extended itself effortlessly from a week prior to Memorial Day in May until one week after Labor Day in September. The ever-responsible Mrs. Moore would suggest an adequate replacement to any abandoned employer who objected to being left without service. In retaliation, more than one attempted to spite her by keeping the replacement on as permanent staff, denying her the ability to return. This, however, was of no concern to her. There was never any shortage of someone else to work for, and it became a well-touted fact that "Mrs. Moore only cleaned her own house in the summertime."

Summers at Fox Lake provided me with a wider exposure to country life. Aside from the lake activities of swimming, boating, and fishing, several small farms nearby provided a close-up look at cows, chicken, horses, and growing field crops. Horse-drawn wagons provided hayrides after dark. During the day, the same wagons were pulled by trucks to roadside markets and grain co-ops where seed grain was sold or traded. In late July and early August, sweet corn, tomatoes, green beans, okra, and other vegetables flooded the farm stands. "Shy Chick" had one of the few deep-water wells that provided water not only for our needs but for those of nearby neighbors who managed to stay on good terms with Bessie Moore. It was my job to pump and carry water and empty slop jars into the ever offensive outhouse. I learned that milk comes from cows, not from bottles or cartons in a store's refrigerated case. Cowpies are neither pies nor do they come from a bakery. Seeing a chick peck its way out of confinement or watching a calf struggle to stand upon unsure legs made the mystery of birth an understandable wonderment. As chickens lost their heads and fish lay gasping in the bottom of a boat, a more complete understanding emerged of what it meant for humans to have a food supply. And so it was that the cycle of life played itself out before my very eyes at Fox Lake, Indiana.

Depending upon Momma Bess's mood, groups of relatives would descend on Shy Chick, which, over the years, evolved to be more modern, complete with indoor running water and toilets. When city folk come to the country, their appetites reflect the size of the city they came from multiplied by the distance they have to travel to reach their country retreat. In the case of Fox Lake, everyone arrived by automobile. And if there had been an airport (which there most certainly was not—at least not within a 50-mile radius of Angola, the nearest town), black folk weren't into flying then.

Even at Fox Lake, Momma Bess had her rituals and insisted on an orderly regimen. I suppose much of this attitude came as a result of running other people's homes on prescribed schedules. Whatever the reason, when family and relatives came to visit, there had to be order to the daily activities. Since most folk were looking to get away from a scheduled life for a few days, it should have been no surprise that many never returned.

As was her habit, breakfast was taken at or before sunrise. It was a light affair with fruit, hot or cold cereal, perhaps a coffee cake, toast, and preserves from the farm stand or, perhaps, one of my mother's vintage Concord grape offerings. This was accompanied by strong hot coffee and one of her three or four daily cigarettes, which were ritualistically smoked after a meal or a cool afternoon libation.

By midmorning, everyone was up and assigned chores. My father was already in with the morning's catch of blue-gills, crappies, perch, and/or a prized small-mouth bass, all gutted and cleaned, ready to become the centerpiece of a bountiful breakfast: beefsteak tomatoes, onions, cucumber salad, smothered country-fried potatoes, some insistent cousin's version of fried or smothered chicken, breakfast ham (parboiled to lessen that wonderful salty preservative), cinnamon buns, and my mother's biscuits, served with peach, apple, grape, or blackberry preserves.

Dinner was another feast of epic proportion. There was more fish, perhaps broiled this time, macaroni and cheese, garlic potato salad, hickory-bark-smoked meats with homemade sauce, freshly picked corn (soaked in water then roasted over hot coals until the husks turned charcoal black, thus flavoring the butter-drenched kernels), hot breads (yeast rolls, cornmeal muffins, or skillet bread), and collard greens (seasoned with the water that had been used to boil the breakfast ham). For dessert, there were various cakes and pies, depending on what expert baker was in attendance—Aunt Ida, Aunt Frankie, Cousin Mary. . . . No matter who did the baking, the results were invariably wonderful.

My contribution, accompanied by several cousins or friends who had made the trip, was pier fishing for young blue-gills, which we lured from their sheltered hiding place under the boats tied up at the dock. Most of our catch was too small to be anywhere near legal size, but how do you tell an excited group of young anglers what "legal size" means? My father always complained that these bite-size morsels were not worth the trouble of scaling and gutting. According to him, by the time all of that was done, there was nothing left to eat. We tried to make up for it by catching frogs, generally found near the swimming area where the reed-choked channel surrounded the beach park. Living side by side with turtles and snakes, the frogs were easy enough to entice with a piece of red cloth on a hook. From there, it was a short hop to the dinner table. In between fishing and hunting, we also had to carry water from the well, transport bags from shopping excursions to the farmer's market, and, sometimes, cut up potatoes for frying.

To a young boy, summer's end came like an uninvited guest, but it was a guest that brought the best gift to the party (on Labor Day). One of my father's early discoveries about the land around Fox Lake was the abundance of hickory trees with notoriously easy-to-peel bark. All real barbecue chefs use hickory wood or chips, but the true experts, like my dad, know that "the best possible results are from the bark only." When burned, the smoke rises and creates a heavenly perfumed cloud that infuses whatever side of meat is being prepared. Once the logs that served as the base of the fire were sufficiently burned down to a bed of coals, soaked hickory bark was added.

More often than not, the meat of choice would be pork, ribs or roast; on occasion, whole pigs on a spit; leg of lamb; and, of course, the ubiquitous "gospel bird" that started out as a "yard bird," the unlucky one in the lot being called into service for Sunday dinner after having its neck snapped and its feathers plucked. After rubbing it down with mixed herbs and condiments at least a day before cooking, the meat went on the fire. But you had to watch it constantly. You wanted the meat to cook with a slow burn, and when the fat from the meat dripped into the wood, the wood would reignite. A good dousing of water from a bucket nearby usually restored calm to the fire and helped keep the meat moist. This almost cold roasting (with essential basting) produced the finest flavor, flavor that went all the way to the bone. Done properly, meat cooked in this fashion has been known to make guests suck the bones until they resembled the same in the desert of Western movies.

Another fall offering was black walnuts. When the nut falls from the tree, it is large and green, about three-quarters the size of a tennis ball. Over time, the outer husk turns dark brown and soft, and the aroma of the husk intensifies, becoming sharp, musky, and fermented. It is at this point that we would spread them out on the floor to be crushed underfoot, revealing the real hard part—the nut itself. Half its original size now, nuts are best left for a few days to dry out (otherwise the walnut juice stains hands, floor, clothes . . . everything), and then the walnut has to be cracked open with a hammer—carefully lest fingers and thumbs become painful targets. The reward inside, waiting to be mined with a pick and patience, was a prize indeed. Meat of the black walnut is especially delicious and flavorful. It is the main ingredient for black walnut ice cream and a variety of cookies and candies.

The walnuts and the barbecue (as well as many other elements of life at Shy Chick) were early lessons in one of life's contradictions, that being that hard work can produce sweet results. The house at Fox Lake is still there, and my entire family continues to enjoy it even though it is no longer possible to spend entire summers there. One thing I know is that those of us who were lucky enough to grow up there had an abundance of experiences that other city-raised children never had. It is these experiences that contributed so much to the man, the father . . . the person I am today. And I feel good about that.

There were always ten to fifteen of us at the lake. Breakfast often ended up as brunch, or a killer breakfast, as we called it. Many of the dishes in this chapter can be enjoyed for breakfast or for brunch. At any time of the day or night, just don't forget to sprinkle the love in while cooking them up.

Derrick Brockman

# Gingered Shrimp, Chicken, and Vegetables with Wild Rice

### INGREDIENTS

1½ pounds medium shrimp, peeled and deveined

4 quarter-size pieces fresh ginger, peeled and finely minced

5 green onions (white and green parts), sliced thin

3 tablespoons dry white wine

1½ tablespoons soy sauce

¾ teaspoon sugar

2 chicken or vegetable bouillon cubes

2 carrots, sliced thin on the diagonal

2 small zucchini, sliced thin on the diagonal

¼ cup olive oil

2 pounds boneless, skinless chicken breasts, cut into cubes

One 6-ounce package wild rice mix

2 stalks celery, sliced thin on the diagonal

1 pound thin asparagus, tough bottoms removed, cut into 1-inch pieces

This recipe will sweep her off her feet! Serve this dish with a side salad and a glass of white wine. Put on your favorite "in the mood" music, light a few candles, and there you are . . . an evening to remember.

1. Combine the shrimp, ginger, half of the green onions, the wine, soy sauce, sugar, and 1 bouillon cube in a medium bowl. Cover and let marinate in the refrigerator for up to 4 hours (at least 1 hour).

2. Steam the carrots and zucchini for several minutes. Add the remaining green onions and crumble 1 bouillon cube over the vegetables while steaming.

3. Heat the olive oil in a medium skillet over medium-high heat and sauté the chicken until almost cooked through.

4. Prepare the wild rice mix according to package directions.

5. Place the marinated shrimp and cooked chicken over the steamer for 5 to 10 minutes. Then mix the shrimp, chicken, carrots, and zucchini in a large saucepan with the celery and asparagus. Cover and cook for 15 minutes or until the rice is done. Serve over rice.

Serves 6

Derrick Malone

# Boozy Black Beans

### INGREDIENTS

1 pound dried black beans, sorted and rinsed

6 cups reduced-sodium chicken broth or water

3 cups chopped onion

½ cup sliced carrots

1 tart apple, peeled, cored, and diced

12 sprigs parsley, tied together with kitchen string

1 cup light rum

1 ounce (1 square) unsweetened chocolate

1 teaspoon dried thyme

1 teaspoon dried basil

2 garlic cloves, crushed

2 teaspoons salt

1 teaspoon black pepper

¼ cup chopped fresh parsley, for garnish

Black beans, also known as turtle beans, are a staple in Latin cuisine. They are a part of Brazil's national dish, feijoada, black beans baked with meat and sausage. As economical as they are good, these kidney-shaped beans with a satiny black skin and a white center are less starchy than their counterparts but are full of protein. High in iron, the black turtle bean has an earthy, sweet flavor with a hint of mushrooms and a creamy texture.

When buying black beans, look for smooth, unshriveled beans. Dried beans are best for this soup, but if you can't find them, canned beans will suffice.

1. In a large bowl, soak the beans overnight in water to cover.

2. The next day, drain the beans. In a soup pot or Crock-Pot, combine the drained beans, broth, onion, carrots, apple, parsley, rum, chocolate, thyme, basil, and garlic. Simmer, covered, for 2 to 3 hours. If using a Crock-Pot, set on medium heat for 8 to 10 hours. When the beans are cooked, discard the parsley. Add the salt and pepper, sprinkle with the chopped parsley, and serve immediately.

Serves 6 to 8

# Devin McCormick
# McWaldorf Salad

### INGREDIENTS

1 cup diced celery

1 large apple, cored and diced

1 cup red or green seedless grapes, cut in half

½ cup walnut or pecan halves

¾ cup mayonnaise

"I like to cook for people I love because it shows them how much I love them. I find it relaxing, but it's really another extension of myself. I learned how to cook from my mother. Dad was always at work, so she did all of the cooking.

"My fondest memories are of my family sitting in the kitchen talking, laughing, and having serious discussions while Mom was rattling some pots and pans. I picked up many things here and there watching her.

"Every summer, one of my uncles would have a family cookout. Most folks do the barbecue, but we would step higher up to the plate and do something different, like fry a turkey. In my family, we're always doing something different, just to express ourselves.

"Activism keeps me busy. My faith and my church give me my real soul food. I like to be involved—to wipe out the so-called stereotypical images of African American men and to give back to my people. This is God's time. I want to pass on this tradition of Real Men Cook. This is one of our legacies that I'm going to continue to pass on to my children."

Mix together all of the ingredients in a medium bowl and refrigerate for 2 hours before serving.

Serves 2 to 4

Note: "I sometimes like to add some pineapple along with a pinch of cinnamon to give me a warm feeling. Goes down like pie!" says Davin McCormick.

## Dr. Cliff West

# The Doctor's Seafood Paella

**INGREDIENTS**

¼ cup fish/seafood seasoning (or you may substitute Mrs. Dash)

1 cup diced onion

3 ears of corn, cut into quarters

¾ cup julienne strips red bell pepper

¾ cup julienne strips green bell pepper

¾ cup julienne strips yellow bell pepper

⅓ cup sliced green onions (green and white parts)

1 cup olive oil

Juice of 1 lemon

One 28-ounce can tomato sauce

½ cup Worcestershire sauce

One 28-ounce can crushed tomatoes

4 cups fresh spinach

2 tablespoons crushed red pepper flakes

4 jalapeño peppers, seeded and sliced

4 white fish fillets, cut into bite-size pieces

½ pound medium shrimp, peeled and deveined, with tails

½ pound scallops

The seminal works of the author, lecturer, and wise and spirit-filled African shaman Malidoma Patrice Somé, *Of Water and the Spirit: Ritual, Magic, and Initiation in the Life of an African Shaman* and *The Healing Wisdom of Africa: Finding Life Purpose Through Nature, Ritual, and Community,* have sustained me in the years since both my sixteen-year-old daughter, Kevani Zelpah Moyo, and dear friend and brother in spirit Dr. Cliff West left this world to dwell among the spirits that are of the "otherworld" that parallels what we humans call living. Kevani and Cliff left us within seventy-two days of each other, between July 9 and September 19, 1999. All but impossible to understand, I still struggle to accept.

The voice of another brother who has been a part of Real Men Cook and knew Dr. Cliff West, Jerry Lacy, joins mine in praise. Read his heart.

"You never know what life is going to deal to you, never! I'm telling you, man, I would have handled that situation differently, even though I had a great time, knowing that that was the last time I was going to cook with you guys! The other day I found a card I got from Cliff; Cliff often wrote cards and brought some kind of food item, hot and spicy, from the trips and seminars he often attended in pursuit of excellence in his profession. I thought it would be too emotional and I threw it away. Memories I have of those times are often overwhelming. We were blessed to have been able to spend those times cooking together."

My children loved Cliff because he made the best guacamole on the planet and his paella was legendary. Might I mention they thought he was way more fun to be with then their "mean old father," but that's another story.—K.K.M.

Combine all of the ingredients (except the spinach, pepper flakes, jalapeños, and seafood) and place in a paella pan or large sauté pan; simmer for 1 hour over medium-low heat. Add the spinach, pepper flakes, and jalapeños and cook for 10 minutes. Then add the seafood and cook for 15 minutes. Add salt to taste. Prepare the rice according to package directions and serve the seafood mixture over the rice.

½ pound mussels,
scubbed and debearded

½ pound squid,
thawed, cleaned, and
rinsed

1 pound crab legs, cut
into 1- to 2-inch pieces

Salt

2 pounds rice

This dish is prescribed by Dr. West to be completely good for the body
and soul! Enjoy!

Serves 8

## Earl Calloway

# Earl Calloway's Deadline Potato Salad

**INGREDIENTS**

3 pounds white
potatoes, peeled and
cut into large cubes

1 cup diced onion

¼ cup diced green bell
pepper

1 tablespoon chopped
garlic

½ cup sweet relish

1 teaspoon fresh lemon
juice

½ cup mayonnaise

¼ cup sandwich spread

1 tablespoon prepared
mustard

Salt

3 hard-boiled eggs,
cut into quarters

Earl Calloway is a reporter for the *Daily Defender*, Chicago's only
African American–owned daily newspaper and one of the oldest
black-owned papers in the country. His journalistic career has spanned
many decades, and he continues to bring stories to the community
with a discerning eye.

This traditional side dish pairs well with James's Fried Chicken (see
page 30). It's quick and easy, and is perfect for a picnic. Your family will
thank you for the recipe and demand you make it for every family
gathering, picnic, birth, and party.

Boil the potatoes in a large pot over medium-high heat for about 20 minutes; drain and let cool. Add the remaining ingredients except the eggs,
mix well, cover, and refrigerate for about 2 hours before serving. Garnish
with the hard-boiled egg quarters.

Serves 8 to 10

Galation Norman

# G Norman's Banana Strawberry Supreme

**INGREDIENTS**

1 package instant
pudding mix (vanilla
or banana-flavored)

One 7-inch angel food
cake

1 pint strawberries,
halved

3 or 4 medium
bananas, cut into
½-inch slices

One 8-ounce container
Cool Whip

This recipe reminds me of a trifle, but simpler. The banana and
strawberry mixture gives a unique flavor to the angel food cake.
Bananas are high in carbohydrates, and both bananas and strawberries
are rich in potassium and vitamin C. Present this supreme dessert on a
beautiful cake platter, and if you are on a first date, or showing off your
culinary prowess to your mate, you will razzle and dazzle her, for sure!

Make the instant pudding according to package directions. Place the
angel food cake on a serving platter. Layer the cake with the strawberries and bananas. Cover with the pudding and top off with Cool Whip.

Serves 6

Greg T. Hinton

# Sautéed Crab Cakes
# with Shrimp or Lobster

**INGREDIENTS**

¾ cup chopped celery

½ cup finely sliced
green onions (green
and white parts)

2 tablespoons butter

1 cup saltine cracker
crumbs

1 teaspoon dry mustard

1 teaspoon Tabasco

Never at a loss for words, Greg—senior director of strategic sourc-
ing and diversity for US Cellular—decided that his strategy in
this instance would be that these cakes speak volumes once you taste
them. Enjoy them as I have on many occasions.

Rémoulade is a classic French sauce that has been adapted by New
Orleans–style cooking. It is a great accompaniment to these gourmet
crab cakes. Make plenty of sauce; they will love you for it.

1. Cook the celery and green onions in the butter until soft; let cool.
In a large bowl, combine the vegetables with the cracker crumbs,

2 teaspoons
Worcestershire sauce

2 eggs, beaten

3 tablespoons chopped
fresh parsley

2 pounds crabmeat,
finely chopped

1 cup finely chopped
shrimp or lobster

¼ cup mayonnaise

2 cups bread crumbs

2 tablespoons
vegetable oil

Rémoulade Sauce
(below)

Lemon wedges

REMOULADE SAUCE

1 cup mayonnaise

2 tablespoons Dijon
mustard

2 tablespoons apple
cider vinegar

1 tablespoon paprika

2 tablespoons prepared
horseradish

1 garlic clove, minced

⅓ cup finely chopped
green onions (green
and white parts)

2 tablespoons chopped
fresh parsley

2 tablespoons ketchup

mustard, Tabasco, Worcestershire, eggs, and parsley; mix well. Add the crabmeat, shrimp, and mayonnaise and combine gently. Using a 2-ounce ice cream scoop, shape the crab cakes into patties and coat with the bread crumbs. Place on a cookie sheet and refrigerate for 1 hour.

2. Heat the oil in a large frying pan and sauté the crab cakes until golden brown, about 3 minutes on each side. Serve with Rémoulade Sauce and a squeeze of lemon.

Makes 20 to 25 crab cakes

## Rémoulade Sauce

Combine all the ingredients, mix well, and serve with crab cakes.

Makes 2 cups

Dr. Horace C. Broy, Jr.

# Sticky Caramel Pecan Rolls

Horace Broy, Sr.; Dr. Horace C. Broy, Jr.; Jamal Broy; Jamal Broy, Jr.

### INGREDIENTS

Two ¼-ounce envelopes active dry yeast

1 cup warm milk

½ cup sugar

¼ pound (1 stick) melted butter or margarine

1 egg

1 teaspoon salt

6 cups flour, plus more for dusting work surface

¼ pound (1 stick) butter or margarine, softened

1 cup packed light brown sugar

2½ teaspoons ground cinnamon

### TOPPING

¼ pound (1 stick) butter or margarine

1½ cups packed brown sugar

1 teaspoon ground cinnamon

1 tablespoon vanilla extract

¼ cup honey

1 tablespoon bourbon

1 to 2 cups chopped pecans

Bake these on a Sunday morning and you will have everyone in your household loving you even more. These also make a wonderful house-warming gift.

1. Dissolve the yeast in 1½ cups luke-warm water in a large mixing bowl. Add the milk, sugar, melted butter, egg, and salt. Mix in the flour, 1 cup at a time. Once the dough reaches a sticky consistency, transfer it to a floured work surface.

2. Knead the dough for about 5 to 7 minutes. Then place it in a lightly buttered bowl and allow it to double in size. Punch the dough in the center and allow it to rest for an additional 10 minutes.

3. Roll the dough into an 18 by 12-inch rectangle; it should be about ¼ inch thick. Spread the softened butter evenly over the surface of the dough. Combine the brown sugar and cinnamon and sprinkle the mixture over the buttered surface. Working carefully, roll the dough like a jelly roll, then cut into 1¼-inch slices.

4. Preheat the oven to 375°F. Spray a 13 by 9-inch pan with nonstick cooking spray.

5. Combine the topping ingredients. Spread the topping mixture over the pan, then place the slices onto the pan close to one another. Let rise for 30 to 45 minutes in a warm, draft-free area until doubled in size.

6. Bake for 15 minutes, or until brown.

7. Remove from the oven, cool slightly while the pan is still very warm, then invert over a platter to release the rolls.

Makes 24 rolls

## Howard Simmons
# Waffles Fantasia

Howard Simmons

**INGREDIENTS**

2¾ cups flour

2 tablespoons sugar

2 teaspoons baking powder

½ teaspoon salt

2 eggs, or substitute Egg Beaters

2¾ cups of 2% milk

1 teaspoon vanilla

¾ cup vegetable oil

There's nothing like waffles on the weekend. What better way to show your mate how much you care than by bringing her breakfast in bed. Don't forget the roses!

1. Sift the flour, sugar, baking powder, and salt together in a large mixing bowl. In a separate bowl, mix together the eggs, milk, vanilla, and oil with an electric mixer. Gradually add the liquid to the dry ingredients and carefully mix the batter. Some small lumps should remain in the batter. Do not overbeat! Let the batter rest for 30 minutes.

2. Preheat a waffle iron to the highest setting; spray with a nonstick cooking spray (even Teflon can use a bit of help sometimes). Scoop the batter onto the waffle iron and cook for 2½ to 3½ minutes, until golden brown.

Makes 6 to 8 waffles

In 1990, for the first production of Real Men Cook, Howard Simmons made more than a thousand waffles using six waffle irons. The waffles had a variety of garnishes, including strawberries, nuts, and whipped cream. He is an award-winning photographer, musician, husband, and proud father—K.K.M.

¼ cup olive oil

¾ cup chopped onion

1¼ cups chopped celery

3 tablespoons minced garlic

¾ cup chopped green bell pepper

¼ cup vegetable oil

½ cup flour

¼ teaspoon black pepper

½ teaspoon cayenne pepper

½ teaspoon Cajun seasoning

1 teaspoon Tabasco or Louisiana hot sauce

Salt

One 16-ounce can tomato sauce

One 16-ounce can diced tomatoes

One 16-ounce can tomato puree

½ cup shrimp base (or a good seafood stock)

1 pound crawfish tails

2 pounds large shrimp, peeled and deveined, with tails

½ cup chopped green onions (white and green parts)

½ cup chopped fresh parsley

## Ira Wilson

# Seafood Viola: Shrimp and Crawfish Etoufée

Etoufée is a thick and spicy stew of fish and vegetables. This Cajun/Creole dish is popular worldwide and is usually served over rice. The term etoufée comes from the French word *étouffer,* "to smother." You may substitute chicken for the shrimp and crawfish. Serve with a nice white wine—then voilà! You will have a magnificent dinner. Ooh la la!

1. Preheat a heavy deep pot (or Dutch oven) over medium-high heat. Add the olive oil, onion, and celery. Sauté for approximately 5 to 7 minutes, until the vegetables are translucent. Add the garlic and green pepper. Continue to sauté for 2 to 3 minutes.

2. Make a dry roux: Heat the vegetable oil in a separate saucepan over medium heat. Add the flour and cook, stirring constantly, until the flour begins to brown. Set aside.

3. Add the black pepper, cayenne, Cajun seasoning, hot sauce, and salt to taste to the sauteed vegetables; continue stirring for 2 minutes. Add the dry roux. Stir in the tomato sauce, diced tomatoes, tomato puree, and shrimp base; continue to stir until all the ingredients are completely incorporated. Reduce the heat to low, cover, and let simmer for 20 minutes. Add the crawfish, shrimp, green onions, and parsley; let simmer for 15 minutes. Serve over rice.

Serves 6 to 8

## Jeff Scales

# Scales's Scrumptious Tropical Rum Coconut Pecan Ice Cream

**INGREDIENTS**

2 eggs

¾ cup sugar

1¾ cups milk

2 cups heavy cream

2 teaspoons vanilla extract

2 teaspoons dark rum

¼ cup shredded unsweetened coconut or coconut flakes

¼ cup pecans, coarsely chopped

This is a sinfully delicious ice cream. It's exotic. Make this for a *very* special occasion.

1. Beat the eggs and sugar with an electric mixer until thick and cream-colored. Add the milk and cook over medium heat until thickened enough to coat a metal spoon. Let cool, then chill overnight.

2. Set up an electric ice cream maker according to manufacturer's instructions. Add the cream and vanilla to the egg mixture and mix well. Pour into the ice cream maker and churn until the ice cream begins to thicken, about 40 minutes. Then remove the lid and add the rum, coconut, and pecans. Continue to freeze until the ice cream is set.

Makes about 4 cups

Kofi Moyo

# Quick Spicy Collards

### INGREDIENTS

1½ cups chopped onion

¼ cup olive oil

2 pounds frozen collard greens

1 jalapeño pepper, seeded and chopped (habañero if you like it really spicy, or scotch bonnet if you Jamaican, mon, or are really adventurous)

½ teaspoon freshly ground fennel seeds

½ teaspoon balsamic vinegar

Lawry's seasoned salt and black pepper

5 garlic cloves, chopped (you won't miss the meat)

¾ cup chopped tomatoes

Here's a quick, healthy, nutritious, and low-cal dish. Enjoy!

Sauté the onion in the olive oil until translucent in Grandma's iron skillet (or whatever you've got). Add the greens, pepper, fennel seeds, vinegar, and salt and pepper to taste. Continue cooking, mixing well. Add the garlic and cook, covered, over medium heat for 15 minutes (that's right, just 15 minutes), turning the greens frequently. Add the tomatoes a few minutes before serving.

Serves 4 to 6

Sam Varnado

# Chef Sam's Tortellini with Capers, Dried Tomatoes, and Black Olives

## INGREDIENTS

1 pound cheese tortellini, refrigerated, frozen, or vacuum-packed

½ cup dried tomatoes

½ cup sliced black olives

½ cup capers, drained

1 small onion, minced

1 cup olive oil

1 teaspoon dried basil

1 teaspoon dried oregano, crushed

½ cup fresh rosemary

Salt and black pepper

Grated Parmesan cheese

Capers are the flower buds of a bush native to the Mediterranean and parts of Asia. They are packed in a vinegar brine and should be rinsed before using to remove the excess salt. They range in size from the petit nonpareil from the southern part of France to larger ones found in Italy. Their piquant flavor marries well with a variety of sauces and condiments.

1. Cook the tortellini al dente according to package directions; drain and set aside.

2. In a medium saucepan, combine the tomatoes, olives, capers, onion, olive oil, basil, oregano, and rosemary, and add salt and pepper to taste. Simmer the mixture for 5 to 6 minutes. Remove from the heat, add the tortellini, and toss. Sprinkle Parmesan cheese over individual servings.

Serves 4

## Walter Payton
# Sweetness Chicken

INGREDIENTS

12 choice pieces chicken (3 to 3½ pounds)

1½ cups orange juice

2 teaspoons dried oregano

½ teaspoon garlic powder

½ teaspoon ground sage

½ teaspoon dried rosemary, crumbled

½ teaspoon dried thyme, crushed

Salt and black pepper

Paprika

¼ cup orange marmalade

1 tablespoon cornstarch dissolved in 2 tablespoons cold water

3 cups hot cooked rice

Orange slices, for garnish

In memory of the late great Walter Payton of the Chicago Bears.

Walter "Sweetness" Payton, out of Jackson State in 1975, wore jersey 34 throughout his professional career with the Chicago Bears. He was voted MVP in 1977 and again in 1985, when the Bears won the Super Bowl. Payton was named All-Pro seven times and played in the Pro Bowl nine times. He was and always will be synonymous with Chicago, a favorite son. Payton played the game with gracefulness, strength, speed, and toughness that put him in a class of his own. His philosophy and dedication to who he was, and all of his accomplishments on and off the field, demonstrate just what it takes to be a "real man." This recipe was one he submitted to Real Men Cook for our 1990 event cookbook..

1. Preheat the oven to 350°F.

2. Place the chicken in a 13 by 9-inch baking dish, skin side down. Combine the juice and seasonings, pour over the chicken, and sprinkle with paprika. Cover and bake for 30 minutes. Turn the chicken and sprinkle with more paprika. Bake, uncovered, for 30 to 40 minutes, until the chicken is tender.

3. Pour the pan juices into a saucepan and skim the fat. Add the marmalade and cornstarch. Cook, stirring constantly, until the sauce is clear and thickened.

4. Serve the chicken with the sauce over a bed of rice. Garnish with orange slices.

Serves 6

## CHAPTER FOUR

# Iron Skillets

I grew up on the South Side of Chicago at 431 West Tremont Street. A wood-frame house, it was just like all the other houses that filled the two city blocks that were Tremont. Sandwiched between the Penn Central Railroad on the east and the B&O line on the west, I doubt that there are many streets in Chicago that are shorter.

In 1945, when I was growing up, the Englewood community was changing. Whites were angrily moving farther south and west in order to separate themselves from "those people," people like my parents, who worked hard and saved enough money to move into decent housing. When my mother found 431 and put a down payment on a house, my father didn't think we could afford it. Nor was he ready for the responsibilities of home ownership, given that he had never owned a home before.

Like most things my father undertook, willingly or not, he mastered his new situation by voraciously reading how-to manuals, *Popular Mechanics* magazines, and library reference books. He then commenced a forty-year vigil to sustain the outward and interior appearance of a well-taken-of home. To this day, although now another family occupies 431, it remains the best-looking house on the block, a block otherwise diseased by urban blight.

Born in coal-mining country—Charleston, West Virginia— my father, Arnold C. Saunders, grew up in a household consisting of his mother and two brothers. He was sandwiched in the middle. He spent thirty years on the Chicago police force but retired never having felt enjoyment at having to carry a gun. Police work was as close as he could get to the law degree he desired. That disappointment and the ugliness of dealing with the results of pressures put upon people locked in the grip of deprivation and poverty made Dad a largely unhappy man.

The thing I remember most about my father was that he was forever fixing things. He was adept at plumbing, electrical work, carpentry, creating things for his hunting and fishing, or just tinkering around in his basement workshop or the garage. Describing himself, he would tell you he was a jack-of-all-trades and master of none. In fact, he reconfigured our house several times over. He enclosed a back porch addition with screening to create a summer refuge from flies and mosquitoes. Its highest and best purpose was as a food locker, in service especially in the winter. He enlarged our living room and added a picture window. My small bedroom was sacrificed for this greater good, but in the end it was a move up in the world for me both literally and figuratively. I went off to the attic, where, next to the photographic darkroom my father had built for my hobby-driven mother, a large bedroom complete with an inside dormer-style window was created for me. He cut a gaping hole in the roof and installed fiberglass insulation and new roofing.

Over the years, he earned the respect of the entire community and was designated "community consultant on all things."

At times, my father spent as much time working on neighbors' houses as he did on ours. The kids on the block brought their broken bicycles, soapbox scooters, and other broken things to Mr.

Saunders's backyard. He could always be counted on to come up with great ideas, including one on how to make a time machine.

In summer, without the annoyance of a school schedule to interrupt our playing, my father would seize the opportunity to have another pair of hands to "hold that light steady" or "hand me the Phillips screwdriver—not the flat one but the one that looks like a cross." It went on for hours. And days. What kind of summer vacation is this? A trip to the hardware store could be arbitrarily demanded right in the middle of a never-ending soft-ball game, just as my turn at bat was coming.

In between projects, a meal for my dad was always some-thing small. He preferred small snacks or sandwiches numerous times a day rather than big meals. Leftovers were a specialty that he rarely left untransformed. The pork chop or piece of beef roast from the previous night's dinner would be cut up with onions, garlic, and peppers and sauced with a roux to become the "Hash of the Day." That was served over potatoes or rice with crusty Italian or French bread, a leftover biscuit, or a quick waffle made from the batter kept sealed in a jar in the refrigera-tor. He would amaze me with how good something could be that started out in the refrigerator looking not at all inviting. A good deal of his creativity was inspired by the work that he hated so. While on his rounds as a police officer ("door shaker" when he was walking a beat), he worked several of the ethnic neighborhoods that Chicago is famous for. Over the years, there were Polish, Italian, Greek, Jewish, and Mexican communities where he became familiar with many of the grocery store, restaurant, and shop owners. Long before such establishments became chi-chi spots with "patio seating" and forty-minute waits, he took lunch with the owners in the back of the store or in the outside receiving area. He would often arrive home with samples of dishes that reflected the diversity of his day. Mexican mole, Italian scaloppini, handmade sausages, Greek pastries, corned beef, and more all found their way to our house on the

South Side. At holiday times, there would be food and wine gifts to be added to our festive holiday tables, enough to feed the multitudes of our familial congregation.

Some of the items Dad brought home did not smell like anything I wanted to eat, especially some of the Polish and Jewish offerings, but as was the rule in our house, when dinner or a meal was served, I had to at least taste some of everything. It was quite a challenge for a young kid whose palate was not yet developed to ingest squid (today's calamari), squash (who wants to eat anything with a name like that? Bugs and worms get squashed!), or asparagus. In spite of my determination to do so, it was hard not to notice that avocados, or alligator pears (now, there's a cool name), when used to make the now popular guacamole, looked like green puke. There were countless other examples, but you get my drift. When I could hold my nose no longer and, under threat of punishment, the mass being chewed had to be swallowed, I would force the foul-tasting villain down. On occasion, the experience was so repugnant that my innards would rebel and I would attempt a run for the toilet, stumbling and with jaws full. When I returned to the table, my reward was a plate of food that was now cold and looked even worse through tears as my parents admonished: "You are *not* wasting food in this house!"

Adding insult to injury, I had to wash dishes with a stomach in turmoil. Table scraps were divided into those for the dog (I would willingly have given him *all* of what was on my plate on those nights) and that which was garbage in the first place. Glasses were always washed first, then silverware, plates, and bowls. Sometimes there were even dessert dishes that I would lick clean when I could get away with it; I'd innocently ask, "Does this have to be washed too?" Pots and pans were last. I would try to convince my parents that they needed to be soaked overnight, but no shortcuts were allowed. Officer Saunders was still sitting at the table reading his paper or another how-to book in preparation for tomorrow's project.

Even though my father was a man of few words, he did talk about work and how to do things that made life easier and more worthwhile. I remember the time Dad dug up an old ten-inch skillet while excavating the backyard to make a concrete foundation for a new garage. He threw it aside to be put into the garbage, but later he reconsidered. He washed the rusted and soil-encrusted skillet and took it into his workroom, where, using a kerosene blowtorch, he burned off all the rust and carbonized grease that gives ironware its characteristic black color. After a second cleansing with strong laundry soap, he took it to the kitchen, boiled water in it, and, after drying, coated it with cooking oil, inside and out. Finally, he put it into a slow oven for several hours. The process of alternately coating and heating was repeated several times, until he was satisfied that the skillet was evenly and completely seasoned.

It was in acts like these that I learned many key values from my father: salvage, utilization, preservation. I learned the importance of conserving and appreciating our resources. I saw how, through the proper application of skills, one could aspire to achieve anything wanted badly enough. Such lessons and values are embodied in the Iron Skillet Award given to men who participate in Real Men Cook.

The recipes in this chapter are great for picnics, large family gatherings, and celebrations—even if there's no reason to celebrate. Just getting together to share good food, fun, and fond memories and create new ones is reason enough. A mean rum punch created by Chef "Sweet" Basil Brathwaite will have your mouth ready for its first sip of paradise while eating some of Ray's Rice Salad or Mean Cabrini Greens. And what would greens be without corn bread? Some say there's a hole in your soul if you don't eat greens with corn bread; Tim's Texas Corn Bread fills that gap. Then end it with something sweet—ah, those Creamy Pecan Pralines. Are there any seconds?

## Al Logan

# Al Logan's Poppie Burgers

### INGREDIENTS

2 pounds finest ground beef available

½ cup diced onion

½ cup finely chopped green bell pepper

¼ cup crushed croutons

2 eggs

3 tablespoons steak sauce

Salt and black pepper

Garlic powder

Al Logan participated in the first Real Man Cook event in 1990. His daughter, Leslye, was one of our first Real Man Cook coordinators. Al was affectionately known to his grandchildren as Poppie. Although deceased in 1995, his memory lives on in the hearts of family, friends, students, coworkers, and others whose lives he touched.

1. Preheat the oven to 350 °F.

2. Combine all of the ingredients in a large mixing bowl, adding salt, pepper, and garlic powder to taste. Form child- or adult-sized patties. Bake for 20 to 30 minutes, depending on the size of the patties. Serve with tossed salad and garlic bread. It's a sure winner with the grandchildren.

Serves 6 to 8

# Anthony Glover

# Sweet and Sour Teriyaki Chicken

**INGREDIENTS**

1 whole chicken
(3 pounds), cut up
into serving pieces

1 cup teriyaki sauce

¼ cup fresh lemon juice

½ teaspoon chopped
garlic

½ tablespoon minced
fresh rosemary

½ cup honey

½ cup vinegar

Salt

"I'm a firehouse cook with grilling skills. I have been doing it for over twenty-three years. I love helping out in the community, working with the other men and their children, and giving them guidance. I learned this from my folks, who are from Monroe, Louisiana, country people who owned and farmed the land.

"My grandfather, my mother and her sisters, uncles and aunts, they all had land; my brother even has 'pine tree land.' Having land is like being the forefathers of a new country.

"We've started a revolution with Real Men Cook, and I am sure that our next generation of children will pick up from us and take it to the next level and become quite successful."

1. Place the chicken pieces, teriyaki sauce, and lemon juice in a resealable plastic bag and let marinate in the refrigerator for 12 to 24 hours.

2. When ready to cook, remove the chicken pieces from the marinade and discard the marinade. Combine the garlic, rosemary, honey, vinegar, and salt to taste with 8 cups water; this is the basting mixture.

3. Heat the grill to low (250° to 275°F). Place the chicken pieces, skin side down, on the grill and cook slowly, turning every 20 minutes and basting with the honey and vinegar mixture, until golden brown, about 3 hours.

Serves 2

**Anthony Glover is a deeply spiritual and community service–minded man, almost to a fault. Always available to every request, ready to cook for every cause. A complex personality, with a unique sense of humor. His spirit and love for his late father is inspiring. He took care of his father when his father became ill. Like all of the brothers, Tony was always there to help, whether it was his own family or someone else's. When off duty, Tony can be found cooking and grilling for the neighborhood.—K.K.M.**

# Charles Sherrell

# Don't Be a Boar Feast

Charles Sherrell

**C**harles Sherrell's culinary efforts showcase a heritage of over twenty-five generations of exceptional oven cookery (baking), which began in the Sherrell family's homeland of Ethiopia and Somalia in northeast Africa.

Sherrell, noted jazz and blues aficionado and radio station owner, is recognized for his distinguished contributions of cakes, rolls, pies, biscuits, and cookies. All who have experienced Sherrell's cooking marvel at what twenty-five generations—more than 1,500 years—have done to bring the world the very best.

Cook the pig and turkey in the oven until done. Cover each with saline solution and sage leaves. Cook the apples in 2 quarts distilled water until boiling occurs, then mash the apples thoroughly. Pour the apple juice over the leaves; let stand and soak for 2 to 3 hours. Place the onions, peppers, cilantro, garlic, tomatoes, salt, pepper, and ½ cup distilled water in a saucepan and heat over medium heat for 3 minutes—this makes a very hot sauce to be enjoyed with the cooked pig and turkey. Serve with a corn bread dressing "American southern style," using a Mississippi coarse-ground cornmeal. Slice the pig and turkey thin. Serve with vegetables such as cooked peas, greens, potatoes, and carrots.

Serves 20 to 25

## INGREDIENTS

One 40-pound wild pig from Zimbabwe

One 16-pound wild turkey from West Virginia

12 large Egyptian sage leaves

12 large apples

10 sweet Georgia onions, finely diced

10 to 12 Jamaican hot peppers, sliced thin

1 bunch cilantro, chopped

4 garlic cloves, sliced thin

6 large tomatoes, diced

1 tablespoon salt

1 teaspoon black pepper

## Chef "Sweet" Basil Brathwaite
# Rum Punch and Pineapple Lemonade

Basil Brathwaite

"Cooking is my life. Most people cook from a book; I cook from my heart and from love.

"My family is from Barbados. My father was a senator, deputy prime minister, and minister of housing and utilities, and with that legacy, I was expected to follow in his footsteps right into politics. Makes sense, right? Wrong. 'Sweet Basil' was a rebellious young man who wanted to do his own thing, mon!

"I left school and went to sea cooking on a ship, where my employer introduced me to a culinary arts program, so I attended the Westminster School of Culinary Arts. I've trained in both the French and British style of cooking.

"After returning to Barbados, I worked in executive positions at the Easterly House and Paradise Club as a catering chef for the royal family. What an honor it was.

"Despite our differences, I used to go back home and spend Father's Day with my dad; being with him still meant a lot to me. So after his passing in 1989, I heard about Real Men Cook on the radio, listening to Chicago radio personalities Bonnie DeShong and Herb Kent, 'the Kool Gent,' talking about Real Men Cook. To this day, I thank God for Real Men Cook, because this event transformed me and gave me purpose to show people just what real men are all about.

"I am inspired by what Real Men Cook does, by raising money for others, and I am blessed and humbled to help them help others."

4 cups sugar

1 cup light rum

One 32-ounce bottle
club soda

1 cup canned
pineapple juice

1 cup canned orange
juice

Juice of 2 limes

One 32-ounce
bottle 7-UP

3 tablespoons
Angostura bitters

One 64-ounce bottle
orange/mango fruit
punch

1 tablespoon grated
nutmeg

Cherries and orange
slices, for garnish

PINEAPPLE
LEMONADE

1 cup sugar

One 16-ounce can
juice-packed pineapple
tidbits

Juice of 3 lemons

4 cups ice water

# Sweet Basil's Rum Punch

1. To make a simple syrup, place the sugar and 4 cups water in a pot over medium heat. Cook until it thickens; let the volume reduce to half of what you started with (about 2 cups).

2. Add the remaining ingredients except the nutmeg and fruit and stir well in a large container that will hold more than 2 gallons. Top off with the nutmeg.

3. Serve over ice and garnish with cherries and orange slices, and a sprinkling of nutmeg.

Makes about 30 drinks

# Sweet Basil's Pineapple Lemonade

Make a simple syrup by boiling the sugar with 2 cups water for 10 minutes. Add the pineapple and lemon juice. Let the juice cool, then strain it and add it to the ice water. Serve over ice.

Makes about 8 drinks

### Cuttie William Bacon III

# Dr. Bacon's Vegan Chili

Cuttie William Bacon III

"**M**y dad, grandpa, and great-grandpa cooked for a living. My uncles ran barbecue places for a living. I'm a fourth-generation cook. My father made his living cooking and waiting tables for very wealthy families in Kentucky. At eight years old, I knew that if I wanted to be wealthy, given the limited opportunities in business for African American men, my best shot was a barbecue pit, a fried chicken place, or a fish place. I did just that—worked my way through college cooking and waiting tables, and at thirty-five, I opened up my first fried chicken and fish place. By thirty-seven, I grossed more than $1 million.

"I've been married twice, and I've had two lovely wives. Both of them say I am a fantastic boyfriend but not a great husband. Cooking is a creative art to me. Food not only has to taste good, it has to look good too. It's my way of impressing African American females so they know that I am not only intellectually smart, but that I have culinary skills as well as an artistic palate.

"I'm a vegetarian and I do most of the cooking because I've worked in restaurants and I know how they are. One tradition in my family is that the Bacon men always cooked much better than the women—with one exception: my son, Cuttie IV. Even my own kids knew that I cooked much better than their mother and were delighted when I had time to cook. Since I was going to school and working two jobs, I didn't often have the time.

"Real Men Cook is a marvelous idea because it brings families out and also gives back to the community. It is an event that gives us a chance to come out and show that we *can*. It also showcases a new image to our boys and young males—and gives them role models that they can emulate. As for the ladies, it shows us in another role—a very positive image. This grand, triple-A, first-class affair is a marvelous idea for Father's Day, as it allows for men to show themselves in a positive image. Being labeled Real Men is a grand idea, because so often we African American males are looked upon as something that's not quite real. But we are, we can do it all . . . Real Men *can!*"

1 pound ground soybean "beef"

One 16-ounce can tomato sauce

One 16-ounce can kidney or chili beans, with liquid

One 16-ounce can whole kernel corn, with liquid

1 cup chopped green bell pepper

1 cup chopped red bell pepper

¼ cup chopped onion

6 tablespoons chili seasoning mix (not chili powder)

Brown the ground soybean "beef" in a large nonstick skillet over medium heat for about 5 minutes. Add the remaining ingredients and continue to cook for 15 to 20 minutes.

Serves 4 to 6

**Cuttie William Bacon III hails from Chicago by way of Kentucky. He is a writer, a public speaker, and an educator, and the father of two children. He's a bon vivant, and a man who embraces life with vigor and humanity.**

# Dr. Carl Bell
## Chinese Chicken Slaw

Dr. Carl Bell

"When I was a little guy, this scientist spirit took hold of me and I would try to bake different things, because, after all, baking is all chemistry. If it didn't turn out right, nobody would know if I had left something out or substituted an ingredient; my fierce, independent, and lone nature wouldn't allow me to tell anyone what I was doing. When I was eleven, I tried baking a marble cake, so I mixed the yellow and chocolate batters and poured them both into a mixing bowl, mixing really well. It came out peanut-butter brown; I didn't know the difference between stirring and folding. I didn't even sift the flour—there was no sifter around—so every once in a while a raw flour ball would explode in your mouth. What an experiment it was!

"When I got to medical school, I was poor. My two roommates were on the GI Bill, so I ended up the chef. I could fry and I did, lots of foods. Vegetables were more challenging—keeping them from drying out—so I experimented once again by adding a little honey to lima beans and peas. And I could fry some pork chops and gravy. My mother was a great cook, and even though I didn't hang out in the kitchen, somehow I learned how to make gravy. As I perfected my talent for frying, I discovered one very important step to frying: the oil had to be hot!

"As a psychiatrist, I see a great deal of dysfunction in our communities as a result of stress and biased societal conditions. Much of my work is dedicated to increasing awareness of how we can relate to one another by removing the barriers or lifting the veil of denial that shields our community from the truth about our mental state.

"Real Men Cook provides a forum for black men to do something constructive and support other men. The association and fellowship at this event give them something to do that is concrete and task oriented, and gives them short-terms goals that they can achieve.

"The cooking and the fellowship support the values and instill the proper 'positioning' of men in the community and clearly demonstrate what it means to be a provider and protector. In essence Real Men Cook shows these guys what it means to be a man. In my profession this is called a corrected emotional experience. It's when you've been away

4 cups shredded green cabbage

2 cups shredded red cabbage

2 cups broccoli florets, blanched

¾ cup finely chopped green onions (green and white parts) (optional)

3 cups cooked, shredded chicken breast meat

1½ cups crispy chow mein noodles (unsalted)

½ teaspoon dry mustard dissolved in ½ teaspoon water

1 tablespoon low-sodium soy sauce

3 tablespoons rice wine vinegar

2 tablespoons hoisin sauce

1 teaspoon ground allspice

1 tablespoon sugar

Salt and black pepper

2 tablespoons Oriental sesame oil

¼ cup extra-virgin olive oil or canola oil

2 cups soybean sprouts (optional)

2 tablespoons sesame seeds, toasted (optional)

from a certain behavior for a long period of time and you take part in something that feels right, it turns the light on for you. Real Men Cook has turned the light on for many of these guys."

1. Combine the cabbage, broccoli, green onions, chicken, and 1 cup of the crispy noodles in a large mixing bowl and toss gently.

2. In a small bowl, whisk together the mustard, soy sauce, vinegar, hoisin sauce, allspice, sugar, and salt and pepper to taste. Whisk in the sesame oil and olive oil until the dressing is emulsified.

3. Pour on just enough dressing to coat the cabbage slaw. Top with the remaining ½ cup crispy noodles and the soybean sprouts and sesame seeds, if using. Serve immediately.

Serves 8 to 10

**Dr. Carl Bell is a psychiatrist and director of the Community Health Council in Chicago. He is married, the father of two, and lives in Chicago.**

## Jerry Lacy
# Bar-B-Q Pot Roast

Jerry Lacy and his daughter,
Chanelle R. Lacy

**INGREDIENTS**

4 to 5 pounds boneless
chuck

1 tablespoon dry onion
soup mix

1 tablespoon minced
fresh parsley

1 tablespoon paprika

Salt and black pepper

1 tablespoon
Worcestershire sauce

⅓ cup dry red wine

1 tablespoon tomato
paste

3 garlic cloves, crushed

2 large carrots, sliced

3 large potatoes, diced

"There were three boys in the family, and my mother insisted that we learn how to wash, iron, and cook. Learning these skills was key to us as single men, then later as husbands and fathers.

"Cooking came to me naturally. I'd watch and help my mother in the kitchen, and I would forever ask questions. The other men in the family would do the smoking or grilling, each with their own 'secret' techniques, and I have some relatives who work in the food industry; one does some catering and the other studied institutional restaurant management.

"When I travel, I like to collect cookbooks, because I am always looking for something different, especially when I am entertaining. When I cook, I consider who's coming and what their tastes might be. I get a lot of pleasure pleasing other people, and once I determine whom I am cooking for and what's on the menu, I can really put together a dinner that's not only good, but memorable. I will go that extra mile to find a unique ingredient to keep it authentic.

"My dear friend Dr. Cliff West was a fun guy—a real riot. He drew me into Real Men Cook and introduced me to Kofi Moyo. The first time I took part in the event, it was real spiritual and I wish I had been involved sooner. But the fact that I did get involved has forever changed my life, thanks to Cliff."

1. Preheat the barbecue grill to medium-low.

2. Place the roast in a heavy foil pan. Combine the soup mix, parsley, paprika, and salt and pepper to taste. Rub the meat thoroughly with the mixture. Add the Worcestershire sauce, wine, tomato paste, and garlic to the pan. Cook for 5 to 6 hours, covered, adding coals as needed to keep the temperature up. If the liquid gets low, add some water. Add the carrots and potatoes during the last hour of cooking.

Serves 8 to 10

## Mark Fishback

# Phi Beta Sigma's Wings with a Ting and a Tang

**INGREDIENTS**

1 cup packed brown sugar

½ cup minced garlic

¼ cup honey

1 cup soy sauce

½ cup Dijon mustard

1 cup vegetable oil

3 pounds chicken wings

The directions say it all. Be prepared to be in the mood, because this dish gives you a little bit of this and a little bit of that. Dancing to the Motown beat, doing those cool Temptations moves, will keep your frat brothers and the sorors coming back for more. You don't have to belong to a fraternity or sorority to enjoy these savory morsels. They are a perfect party dish. Party on and on all night long, or as long as they last!

First, put on your favorite Temptations CD or album . . . Eddie, David, Melvin, Paul, Otis, Dennis—you know the originals.

Second, heat the grill accordingly.

Third, place all of the marinade ingredients into a large bowl and toss. Yo! Easy on the honey, you don't want it too sweet. The tang is what hits 'em.

Apply the marinade with a basting brush to each piece of chicken. Place the chicken over medium heat. Turn the chicken so that it cooks evenly and not too fast. Cook for 45 minutes, or until desired doneness.

Fourth, serve this to your family, friends, frat brothers, and sorors, and watch their eyes light up after one bite.

Serves 6

Note: The vegetable oil will allow the marinade to hold and not burn in the grill heat.

Ray Glend

# Ray's Rice Salad (Sprinkled with Love)

**INGREDIENTS**

2 cups wild rice

1 cup long-grain brown rice

2 bunches cilantro, chopped

1 bunch parsley, chopped

2 green onions (green and white parts), chopped

⅓ cup chopped celery

1 cup pecan halves, toasted

Raspberry vinaigrette salad dressing (store-bought)

Bragg Liquid Aminos

¼ cup olive oil

This is a wonderful salad to serve at room temperature. It's great for vegetarians. Using Bragg Liquid Aminos, a liquid protein concentrate derived from soybeans, is a healthy alternative to soy sauce or tamari. Look for it in your local health food store. The raspberry vinaigrette blends with the nutty flavors of the wild and brown rice to create an exotic taste. This can serve as a side dish with your favorite Real Men Cook entrée.

1. Cook the rice according to package directions, let cool, and place in a large bowl.

2. In another bowl, combine the cilantro, parsley, green onions, celery, and pecans, and add to the rice.

3. Moisten the rice mixture with raspberry vinaigrette and liquid aminos to taste (make sure it's not too wet or too dry), then add the olive oil.

Serves 6

Note: Pine nuts or walnuts may be substituted for the pecans. Most health food stores and some grocery stores carry Bragg Liquid Aminos. Sprinkle with love, before and after. Enjoy!

# Richard Blackmon, Jr.
# Mean Cabrini Greens

**INGREDIENTS**

3 pounds fresh collard greens

1 pound smoked turkey wings or legs

1½ cups chopped onion

3 garlic cloves, chopped

2 tablespoons butter

1 tablespoon Lawry's seasoned salt

"My uncle Moody was from the South and he did a lot of cooking. He was the kind of uncle who taught you things that no one else wanted you to know. Although my mother raised me, he was a real presence in my life. He was the man I took my first drink with and went to my first gambling house with. He loved cooking and did all of the cooking in the house. In our culture, cooking means more than just good food. I can remember Uncle Moody was cooking a coon stew (raccoon). It had sweet potatoes, vegetables, and everything. But I couldn't help looking at it like it was a dog. It was probably seasoned just right, and it did smell good. Young or not, I knew this was something that I didn't want to eat, and thankfully, my mother called me to come on home in the nick of time. This man was full of life. To put him in perspective, he had a truck he called the Salty Dog. That was Uncle Moody. He was definitely a force in my life and I gravitated to everything he did, because he just enjoyed everything, enjoyed life.

"As parents, sometimes we get so caught up in what kids should know in order to do the right things, we often forget to help them do the natural things.

"Real Men Cook has a whole other connotation for me. It means that real men get up and do what they're supposed to do. Fatherhood for some is something that has been put on the back burner, like it's optional. Manhood is not optional.

"Father's Day 2000 was a turning point for my family. I wanted custody of my son, who was having difficulty at school. Well, he joined me at Real Men Cook the first year I participated. He went home and told his mother how proud he was of me and the event, and she gave me custody of him. That was a major turning point in my life. What that experience did for me and my kids meant more than the time and the money that we invested. My family has never been the same."

1. Clean the greens by removing excess stems from the leaves, and inspect thoroughly for insects and damaged leaves. Wash thoroughly in cold water until the water runs clear.

2. Remove the turkey meat from the bones. Place the turkey and 1 cup water in a large pot. Add the onion, garlic, and butter and bring to a boil. Reduce the heat and let simmer for 5 minutes, then add the greens; add more water if necessary. Sprinkle the seasoned salt directly on the greens. Cook, covered, over medium heat for 30 to 40 minutes, until tender. Serve with hot sauce, hot peppers, and a piece of corn bread.

Serves 5 to 7

## Rick Mays
# Monsieur Rick's Blackened Salmon

"I like cooking because I enjoy taking the raw ingredients and putting them together—like an artist starts out with a blank canvas and comes out with a picture—then presenting it to someone.

"I've got to credit my dad for my knowledge of good food. Dad was a good cook, and he was a waiter on a railroad dining car. He also worked at the restaurant in the Chicago Union Stockyards called the Sirloin Room, in the Stockyard Inn Restaurant, one of the finest steak houses in the country. I went to work sometimes with my dad, and he'd show me how to set the table, fold the napkins, and bus the tables. By the time I was sixteen, following in my dad's footsteps, I was waiting tables part-time at the same restaurant. He insisted that all of us, my sisters and my brothers, learn how to cook.

"I passed that requirement down to my sons. They would come up with the menu idea, and then not only would we go about preparing it, but we'd go to the grocery store, where they learned how to go shopping. Dad also taught us how to shop: he showed us how to pick out meats, check the date and check the prices, and spot a good deal or a bad one. From the planning to the preparation to the finished product, I've taught my kids just like my dad taught me.

## INGREDIENTS

3 pounds salmon fillets or steaks

½ pound (2 sticks) butter, melted (margarine is not recommended)

One 2-ounce bottle Chef Paul Prudhomme's Blackened Redfish Magic seasoning

"What I like most about Real Men Cook is that it gives to the little guy—the smaller not-for-profit agencies that don't have the big pocketbook. These organizations have to struggle to get dollars on a regular basis, and this benefit was, and continues to be, a shot in the arm and a positive reflection on the African American community. This is pitching in, not a handout—it's giving someone a helping hand. If you have to question why people participate, then you're not even the right person to participate. In fact, you're not even the right person to attend, but I encourage you to. This changes you; it's a year-round good feeling that starts on Father's Day and continues until the next year."

1. Place the salmon skin side up and brush with melted butter. Shake on the seasoning until it completely covers the fish. Take the remaining melted butter and lightly drizzle over the salmon.

2. Place an iron skillet or griddle directly on top of the hot coals, inside of the grill, for approximately 5 minutes. Put the salmon, skin side down, in the hot skillet and place the top on the grill. Turn with a spatula after about 3 to 4 minutes and cook on the other side for 2 to 3 minutes. (If using salmon steaks, which are thicker, grill for 3 to 5 minutes per side; butter and season before turning.) Test for desired doneness. Remove and serve.

Serves 6

**Rick Mays is one of the many ambassadors of Real Men Cook. He's one of those who have been there basically from the very beginning. He has cooked, volunteered, worked with the organizers, and stepped in when needed, including helping with this book. I am grateful for his friendship and kinship to the mission of Real Men Cook.—K.K.M.**

## Roland S. Martin

# Roland S. Martin's Texas Spaghetti

### INGREDIENTS

1½ pounds spaghetti

2 tablespoons olive oil

1 pound ground beef

1 pound Italian sausage links (turkey or beef sausages may be substituted)

¾ cup chopped onion

¼ cup sliced green onions (green and white parts)

½ bunch parsley, chopped

½ cup chopped celery

1¼ cups chopped green bell pepper

2 tablespoons Tony Chachere's Creole Seasoning or Lawry's seasoned salt

½ tablespoon garlic powder

½ tablespoon Mrs. Dash Original Blend

Two 16-ounce cans tomato sauce

One 18-ounce bottle Kraft Honey Barbecue Sauce

"Sorry, Momma, your spaghetti never tasted this good."

1. Of course, the first thing you have to do is boil the spaghetti. Once done, drain under cold water, toss with the olive oil, and set aside.

2. Brown the ground beef in a large skillet over medium-high heat. Broil the Italian sausages in a 375°F oven until they are crispy brown. Remember to rotate the sausages so that they cook evenly.

3. Add the onion, green onions, parsley, celery, green pepper, and seasonings to the ground beef; continue to cook to your satisfaction.

4. Remove the sausages from the oven, cut them up into 2-inch pieces, and add to the pan of ground beef mixture. Pour in the tomato sauce and barbecue sauce and bring to a boil, then reduce the heat and cook for 10 minutes, stirring constantly. It's best to keep the meat sauce and the spaghetti separate. To serve, place some spaghetti on a plate and top with some meat sauce.

Serves 10 to 12

Note: When making this recipe, you will surely taste the flavor of the barbecue and how much sweeter your spaghetti will taste. The Italian sausages will add a whole different dimension, making your spaghetti the talk of your home or office for its different twist.

**Roland S. Martin is a nationally acclaimed journalist, syndicated columnist, and founder of an Internet news company. He was recently named executive editor of the *Chicago Daily Defender*.**

# Terrence Davis
# Creamy Pecan Pralines

INGREDIENTS

One 12-ounce can
evaporated milk

2 cups sugar

¼ pound (1 stick) butter
or margarine

1 teaspoon vanilla
extract

2 cups chopped pecans

"As a young boy growing up in New Orleans, I remember that we were always out in the yard with our father. Whether it was barbecue on the grill or whether we were frying something—a turkey or catfish—or boiling crawfish, crabs, or shrimp, we were all out in the yard cooking. It's something that I remember as always being a source of pride for the men in our families, and that there was a sense of competitiveness about who had the best food and who could cook the best. You know with New Orleans, food is big, and a lot of pride is taken in the preparation of food and people enjoying good food.

"When I am at the barber shop, there's always good conversation or some wisdom shared. I remember a few days after Thanksgiving the guys started talking about their fried turkeys, about what they did with their turkeys and how you had to inject them with seasoning, and you had to create these different seasoning packets. I mean they were trying to hint about how they did it without revealing their secrets. Then there was a good dose of male competitiveness, where the guys were claiming bragging rights, yours couldn't be better than mine. It got to the point where they stopped by each other's houses to taste these masterpieces.

"In New Orleans, we like to entertain and come together and socialize. It's been passed down from generation to generation. We like for people to come over and eat and be merry and satisfied. Guess that's why they call it the Big Easy.

"I have two cousins. We call them 'the Joshua Boys,' two of the best backyard cooks in New Orleans. Every time there's a function or something going on at church, they bring these guys in and they fry the best chicken and fish that you will have, right in the backyard. Both are firefighters, but you'd swear they were professional chefs. I can taste it now. Rich foods are one of my weaknesses."

1. Line a cookie sheet with buttered waxed paper.

2. Combine the milk, sugar, and butter in a large saucepan over medium heat. Stir frequently to avoid sticking. When the mixture begins to boil,

add the vanilla and reduce the heat. Stir the mixture until it becomes thick and turns caramel in color, about 20 to 30 minutes. Stir in the pecans.

3. Spread the mixture evenly onto the cookie sheet. Allow the pralines to cool until they harden. Cut into squares and serve.

Makes 16 to 20 pieces

## Tim Dillinger
# Tim's Texas Corn Bread

**INGREDIENTS**

2 cups self-rising cornmeal

1 teaspoon salt

3 tablespoons sugar

1 cup sour cream

One 8-ounce can cream-style corn

1 large onion, finely diced

1 medium green bell pepper, diced

1 jalapeño pepper, diced

3 eggs, beaten

¾ cup corn oil

3 tablespoons vegetable shortening

Two 8-ounce packages grated sharp Cheddar cheese

Serve this corn bread with some greens and a salad. This is good eating!

1. Preheat the oven to 350°F.

2. In a large bowl, combine all of the ingredients except the shortening, cheese, and ¼ cup of the cornmeal. Mix well.

3. Place the shortening in a 9-inch black iron skillet and melt it over low heat. While the shortening is bubbling, sprinkle a thin layer of the reserved cornmeal on the bottom and sides of the skillet and let it brown lightly. Remove from the stove and sprinkle a layer of cheese on the bottom of the skillet. Pour a layer of batter over the cheese. When the cheese is covered, sprinkle in another layer of cornmeal, then repeat with the cheese. Pour in the remaining batter and sprinkle a final layer of cheese on top.

4. Bake for 50 minutes. Let cool for 15 minutes before removing from the skillet.

Serves 8

## Undrae Winding
# Gianan's Delight

### INGREDIENTS

1 pound angel hair pasta

3 tablespoons vegetable oil

2 cups grated green cabbage

⅓ cup grated carrots

10 ounces country smoked sausage

10 ounces boneless, skinless chicken breasts, chopped

10 ounces medium shrimp, peeled and deveined

5 ounces crabmeat (lump, snow, or king crab, your choice), chopped

5 ounces cooked lobster meat, diced

Soy sauce

Cabbage is no stranger to our diet. Other members in the cabbage family are brussels sprouts, broccoli, cauliflower, and kale. It can be cooked in a variety of ways or eaten raw in a good coleslaw. It contains vitamins A and C. Smother it, sauté it, even boil it; no matter how you fix it, just eat it, because it's very good for you.

1. Boil the pasta until it is about 95 percent done. Drain under cold water and set aside.

2. Heat the vegetable oil in a large sauté pan. Stir-fry the cabbage and carrots for 3 to 4 minutes over high heat, remove from the pan, and set aside. Add the sausage and chicken to the sauté pan and cook until almost done. Add the shrimp, crab, and lobster to the sauté pan and continue to cook until the meat and seafood are done. Return the cabbage mixture to the pan, add the pasta, and season the entire mixture to taste with soy sauce.

Serves 6 to 8

# Walter Cannon

# Stop-Fighting-in-That-Line Shrimp and Broccoli Casserole

**INGREDIENTS**

2 tablespoons olive oil

2 pounds medium shrimp, peeled and deveined

1½ tablespoons Lawry's seasoned salt

1 tablespoon garlic salt

2 teaspoons lemon-pepper seasoning

2 cups chopped broccoli florets

1 pound noodles (your favorite shape)

Three 10¾-ounce cans condensed cream of mushroom soup

One 8-ounce package shredded Cheddar cheese

"My mom had three boys, and I'm the youngest. I was always in the streets—here and there. She feared that I would never get married, so she made sure that I knew how to cook, clean, work hard, and save. Well, I took those sage words to heart and I've been cooking for over thirty years. It relaxes me, and frankly, I love it.

"Being a single parent of two great kids, a son and a daughter, the first year was challenging, and there was a lot for all three of us to learn. When I got involved with Real Men Cook, it made a difference in my relationship with my kids. It made it stronger, bringing us much closer. Perhaps they saw the other men performing multiple tasks as well as the bonding and fellowship that are an integral part of this event.

"One of my favorite recipes to cook is Broccoli and Shrimp Casserole. It is my signature dish. People ask, what is it that sets it apart from other casseroles? You mean there really *are* other casseroles? It's the seasoned salt and the Caribbean spices. All of what they say about the pushing and shoving is true. Sounds like a story, but it is true."

1. Preheat the oven to 350°F. Butter an 8 by 8-inch casserole dish.

2. Oil a ceramic bowl, then combine the shrimp, seasoned salt, garlic salt, and lemon-pepper seasoning. Set aside.

3. In a 3-quart saucepan, steam the broccoli for 15 minutes. In a separate pot, cook the noodles according to package directions.

4. In the casserole dish, make a layer of noodles, then of broccoli, then add the shrimp; cover with the soup and sprinkle the Cheddar cheese on top. Cover with aluminum foil and bake for 35 minutes.

Serves 6 to 8

# CHAPTER FIVE

# Wooden Spoons and Cake Bowls

Among the other blessings at 431 West Tremont was a cherry tree, planted in the backyard when my mother and father bought that first house. That tree became a gathering place for children from blocks around, and after careful cultivation over a period of seven years, it followed the divine path of fruit trees by reaching maturity and providing fruit that went into pies (deep-dish, crunch, lattice-top, and cobblers) and wine. We had cherry wars with pits and stems everywhere. The birds of course had their share.

Eventually, Dad was forced to cut the tree down. As the kids in the neighborhood got bigger and their numbers grew, they would ignore invitations to wait for the ripened fruit. Midnight raiders repeatedly broke the branches and made a mess of the backyard, so, after much consternation, Dad did the George Washington thing and laid waste to the source of our cherry pie pleasure.

Of course, there was still plenty more sweet stuff traditional to the African American kitchen. Cane syrup ended up on lots of things. The brand name Alaga combines the abbreviations of Alabama and Georgia and is popular among people from the South, where cane syrup carried regional names. When Alaga was mixed with butter on a plate, there was serious "sopping" to be done. (Do I have to define "sop"?) There was also maple syrup, packaged in a tin. Even though maple syrup cost more than cane, it was thin and watery. We kids called it "white folks' syrup." It was a taste one grew to appreciate as tastes matured. Generally, it was preferred on Momma's waffles, surpassed only by a gourmet brand purchased by mail order or presented as a holiday gift from someone who had been "out east" (Maine, Vermont, or upstate New York). I have never been a fan of molasses, even when Brer Rabbit told us it was "good for you—plenty of iron to make you strong." I messed up my waffles with the stuff once and had to eat them anyway. ("Waste not, want not!")

In a pinch, we made our own syrup when the store-bought version ran out or developed mold because someone had contaminated it with butter or margarine by sticking a spoon or knife into the bottle. The mold floated on the surface like a jellyfish, tainting the flavor. In our house, we called the unsightly growth "Mother"—for reasons that I cannot recall.

Our next-door neighbor, Mrs. Martin, was the syrup-making queen. With three boys in her house plus my frequent visits, short work was always made of even the quart-size bottle of Alaga. We used it to slather the rolls and other hot breads found in abundance in her kitchen. When we ran out, her answer was to whip up a quick, homemade batch of iron-skillet syrup. By caramelizing some sugar with a little water, butter, and vanilla flavoring, we had syrup in no time at all.

Waffles were a constant fixture in my house. My mother's waffles were the subject of constant praise from all who ever had the opportunity to breakfast with us. Sweet enough to eat without the butter and syrup, her waffles demanded adding weight lest they float right off the plate. The secret? She always folded her beaten egg whites into the batter just before she poured it onto the iron. Sometimes she employed two large waffle irons simultaneously when there was an extra mouth or two at the table. On occasion, when time was short or Mom didn't want to watch the waffles while everyone else was eating them, there would be biscuits. That was fine for us kids but not for Officer Saunders. Generally, my father found the biscuits too short. Or there was too much shortening, lard, or even Crisco (the solid vegetable shortening). The biscuits just never seemed to suit "Mr. Biscuit," Arnold Saunders. I could barely tell the difference in taste, but I do have to say that my father consistently made an extra-large variety. He called them "hoecakes" and felt "the bigger, the better."

The bread wars notwithstanding, Momma was a very good cook. Her repertoire was quite extensive, including fried corn, smothered potatoes, pasta dishes (spaghetti, in those days), fried chicken, squirrel, fish, chicken and dumplings, cakes, candy, lemon pie. Her proficiency in the kitchen could be matched only by her passion for seeking education. Momma studied everything under the sun: ceramics, photography, lapidary and jewelry making, travel agency certification, real estate brokerage, wine making . . . I am sure there were other courses that I have forgotten. Daddy built an array of things to support Momma's hobbies: an electric kiln for firing ceramic projects; a workbench for lapidary projects; shelves for barrels and bottles of grape, raisin, apricot, peach, and elderberry wine.

During summers, on any given Saturday morning—real early, just when you thought you were going to get that extra snooze time that going to school robs you of—Momma would announce a trip to Michigan "to get her grapes." What that meant was that not only that Saturday but all subsequent weekends would be devoted to the production of wine. It began with washing, picking through, mashing, sugaring, watching, pouring, straining, mixing, testing, more watching, and finally—racked with anxiety—bottling. This final process required sterilizing bottles and corks enough to accommodate thirty to forty gallons of grape, elderberry, peach, strawberry, apricot, or whatever was ready to be labeled, stored, and given as holiday gifts. All of this was at the expense of a teenage boy who was much more interested in late-night hanging out with friends and a newfound interest in the opposite sex. At least her wine-making hobby introduced me to one of my own: sampling wine that had matured to near lethal potency in Momma's big oak barrels.

The fall ushered in a harvest of pumpkin, butternut, acorn, and a variety of other winter squash that was customarily roasted to intensify flavor. It was served with butter, cinnamon, or nutmeg; boiled and whipped with eggs, butter, and cream and baked again soufflé style; or made into various custards and pies. The crisp, dry days of fall were also times for walking tours along dirt roads that ran between farmhouses and lakes that dotted the back roads of Steuben County. Keeping a careful eye out for snakes, my mother had a knack for spotting areas likely to lead us to wild raspberry and blackberry picking. Deep-dish cobbler was the reward on days like these, fruit pies and cobblers being fundamental to fall dessert making.

It is a sad world indeed as I stand as witness to an all-too-commonplace travesty: the use of canned fruit in pies and cobblers. All across this country, restaurants and alleged down-home cooks are using canned peaches in heavy syrup to make what amounts to faux peach cobblers and deep-dish pies. Fortunately, my memory can transport me back to other days. I can taste the corner pieces of my mother's cobbler, where there was an abundance of flaky crust, saturated with sugary berry filling, some of which bubbled to the top and over the side, where the sugar got a little burned, thus cementing the crust to the glass Pyrex dish. I remember working up a sweat of anticipation as I tried to get the entire corner out of the dish and into my bowl.

Personally, I have not as yet mastered the fine art of baking. But I was raised by people who cared enough about baking to forgo the use of canned fruit in pies. No matter the seasonal conditions, other alternatives to canned fruit were used: reconstituted dried fruit, fresh frozen, or even a seasonal basket from the South or Southwest are all good alternatives, just never—ever—canned.

To my fellow readers, please make note that the recipes and stories in this chapter are truly consistent with the title "Wooden Spoons and Cake Bowls." The skills of the cook are tantamount to their success, meaning they have to come out right. Baking is as much science as it is art. All of these dishes are heritage recipes—all sweet. They speak to where they come from, the family.

Bluesman Fernando Jones puts us in the mood with his Special Sweet Potato Pie; dare we not have this traditional pie on the table during the holidays? Throw that thought right out of your mind. What about a pound cake? No table would be worth the wood it is made of without having a delicious sour cream pound cake to enjoy. Better yet, there's a bread pudding recipe to savor. And ah, yes, Chef Michael Seay's Famous Flourless Chocolate Cake and Eugene Morris's Chocolate Marble Cheesecake are for the chocolate lover in you. Save some extra room for these delicious delights.

# African American Foodways: Traditions and Facts

Some people like to think of the popular concept of "soul food," "comfort food," "African American cooking," and "African American foodways" as a development that took place at some period in America. I and many others choose to look to our respective motherland, the source of our earliest beginnings. We can look as far back as 6,000 B.C., when black people in Africa were living in urban farming communities, had developed cotton and oil-producing plants, and had introduced them to the Egyptians and ultimately to the world.

These African communities grew rice, millet, sorghum, peanuts, watermelon, and other food products. Agronomists have traced the origin of such staple crops as rice, sorgo, various species of millet, and two species of yams, and oil-producing plants such as the oil palm and sesame, to West African centers.

A review of West Africa from the sixteenth through the eighteenth century, the region and period from which most present-day African Americans can trace their ancestry, reveals long-standing production of foods such as okra, cassava, pigeon peas, kidney beans, black-eyed peas (cowpeas), peanuts (groundnuts), eggplants (guinea squash), onion, maize (Indian corn), tomatoes, hot peppers, spinach, cabbage, sweet potatoes, and others. West Africans enjoyed fruits such as sweet fig bananas, watermelons, and a variety of other melons.

Besides what they grew, the Africans used nets or spears to catch shrimp, cod, pike, flounder, sole, lobster, crab, carp, eel, mackerel, alligator, and varieties of fish that were unknown in America and Europe.

With flour, cinnamon, sugar, butter, and other ingredients, they made a variety of cakes, puddings, pies, and candy. A special pie was made with cooked mashed beans that is still prepared and enjoyed today by many African American families.

They seasoned their foods with special blends of peppers, sauces, herbs, and spices, and prepared them in various types of cooking equipment, including a special earthen vessel that resembles a double boiler.

*by Howard Paige*

**Howard Paige began researching African American foodways more than twenty years ago. He has written three books, conducts lectures, and performs food demonstrations across the country. For the past twelve years, Mr. Paige has presented African American Foodways demonstrations at the Henry Ford Museum, in Dearborn, Michigan. He has been an adviser to the Anacostia Museum of the Smithsonian Institution. Mr. Paige is recognized as one of the foremost experts on African and African American food traditions.**

Jimm Cobb

# Jimm Cobb's Carrot Cake

Jimm Cobb

### INGREDIENTS

2 cups sugar

1½ cups vegetable oil

4 eggs

2½ cups flour

1 teaspoon ground
cinnamon

2 teaspoons baking
soda

1 teaspoon salt

3 cups grated or
shredded carrots

½ cup chopped nuts

Cream Cheese Frosting
(below)

### CREAM CHEESE
FROSTING

One 8-ounce package
cream cheese

1-pound box
confectioners' sugar

¼ pound (1 stick) butter

2 teaspoons vanilla
extract

According to food historians, today's carrot cake is descended from medieval carrot puddings. History tells us that carrots date back more than two thousand years and are known for their healthful properties. They are high in carotene and renowned for the potency of their vitamin A. They are a member of the parsley family. Plan to make two of these cakes, one for you and the other to share with friends.

1. Preheat the oven to 325°F.

2. Combine the sugar and oil in a large bowl and mix together with an electric mixer until fluffy. Add the eggs and continue to mix. Sift together the flour, cinnamon, baking soda, and salt and add to the mixture. Mix in the carrots and nuts.

3. Pour the batter into a 13 by 9-inch cake pan and bake for 50 to 55 minutes. (This recipe will also make two 9-inch layers, but the baking time will be less.) Let cool, then spread frosting on top. Cut into squares.

Serves 6 to 8

## Cream Cheese Frosting

Mix the cream cheese, sugar, and butter until creamy. Add the vanilla and continue to mix. If the icing is too thin, add more sugar until it's the right consistency for spreading.

Note: One drop each of red and yellow food coloring makes a nice pale orange color for icing.

Avell Collier

# Mr. C's Bread Puddin'

Avell Collier

Whether it's bread pudding with a *g* or without, bread puddin', no matter how you spell it, is just darn good.

1. Preheat the oven to 350°F.

2. Place the eggs, sugar, nutmeg, butter, condensed milk, and whole milk in a large bowl. Beat the ingredients well with a large spoon. Fold in the bread cubes and continue to stir until well mixed. Pour into a 9 by 9-inch baking dish and bake 40 minutes, or until the pudding is firm.

Serves 6 to 8

**INGREDIENTS**

4 eggs

2 cups sugar

1 teaspoon grated nutmeg

½ pound (2 sticks) melted butter

1 cup sweetened condensed milk

2 cups whole milk

6 cups French bread cubes, refrigerated overnight

### Chef Michael Seay
# Chef Michael's Famous Flourless Chocolate Cake

Chef Michael Seay

"I was born into a family of cooks. At six years of age I started cooking with my mother in Louisville, Kentucky, where she owned a catering company. I decided early on that this would be my vocation and avocation. But my folks wouldn't allow me to pursue my love for cooking because I was from a family that expected me to go to college. Cooking satisfies my passion for creativity and aesthetics. Simply put, I love and enjoy food.

"I am the chef and owner of All Seasons, Inc., and the Peacock Café at the NBC Tower in Chicago. Serving the best means quality for my patrons. I get up before dawn, and get down to the market to touch, taste, and feel what I am cooking. I want to see the quality of what I am buying—from the chain stores to the ethnic stores sprinkled throughout Chicago—Jamaican, African, Chinese. I keep it real and authentic.

"Europe has always regarded this profession with the highest esteem. It wasn't until the 1970s and '80s that Americans took note of what chefs and food were really all about. Then came the '90s and the Food Network, and cooking really took off and became entertainment. Black folks have always been involved with food. They cooked for the people they worked for, and for the people who owned them.

"Southern cuisine, as I see it, is food that had its origins with black people. Originally, in this country it meant so-called soul food: what we ate on a regular basis that derived from slavery, like chitterlings and the cheapest cuts of meat. We knew how to make the best dishes from the cheapest meats and leftovers. We must always present ourselves in the positive, like we do in Real Men Cook. It's about coming together and sharing stories, ideas, and recipes for living."

1. Preheat the oven to 250°F. Butter a 10-inch springform pan and dust with flour, tapping out the excess.

2. Gently melt the chocolate and butter in a small saucepan over low heat (or microwave on low power); let cool slightly. Beat the egg yolks, 4 tablespoons of the sugar, and the orange liqueur for about 5 minutes

½ pound semisweet
chocolate

¼ pound (1 stick)
unsalted butter

8 eggs, separated

7 tablespoons sugar

⅓ cup orange-flavored
liqueur, such as Grand
Marnier

¾ teaspoon cream
of tartar

Pinch of salt

Ganache (below)

Sweetened whipped
cream, for garnish

GANACHE

1 pound semisweet
chocolate

1 cup heavy cream

with a whisk or an electric mixer. Fold in the chocolate mixture and mix
thoroughly.

3. Beat the egg whites, cream of tartar, and salt in a large, clean,
grease-free mixing bowl until foamy. Divide the beaten egg whites into
two bowls. In one bowl, gradually beat in the remaining 3 tablespoons
sugar, beating well after each addition. Then add the chocolate mixture;
continue to beat. Gently fold in the remaining egg whites.

4. Transfer the batter to the prepared pan and bake for 1½ to 2 hours,
turning every 30 minutes. Let cool completely before removing the cake
from the pan, then set it on a wire rack. Completely cover the cake with
warm ganache. Serve garnished with a dollop of whipped cream.

Serves 12

## Ganache

1. Chop the chocolate into small pieces. Bring the cream just to a boil,
stirring to prevent scorching. (Use the freshest cream available; old
cream is more likely to curdle when it is boiled.)

2. Add the chocolate to the cream. Remove from the heat, stir, and let
stand for a few minutes. Stir again until the chocolate is completely
melted and the mixture is smooth. If necessary, warm gently over low
heat to completely melt the chocolate. At this point, the ganache is
ready to be used as an icing or glaze. Apply it by pouring it over the
cake.

**I've known Chef Michael Seay for over thirty-five years. When we
first met, there was a great admiration and connection between us,
and then some ten years later I found out why we bonded: we were
cousins—blood relations! Michael is dedicated to his profession. He
wakes up and goes to sleep cooking, and you always see him in his
starched white chef's uniform. You don't come half-stepping in his
kitchen to work. It's serious and at the same time it's an honor to
watch him create one of his culinary masterpieces. Cooking is more**

than a passion for him; it's in his blood. He has his mome
when he turns it out—it'll be right.

Recipes are just guides for those unsure of what life has to
offer; cooking is an inspiration and passion. Few embody the
spirit more than Chef Michael Seay. Thank you for your passion!
—K.K.M.

## Chef Michael Johnson

# Sour Cream Pound Cake

**INGREDIENTS**

¾ pound (3 sticks)
butter, softened

2¾ cups sugar

1 teaspoon vanilla
extract

6 eggs

2 cups flour

½ teaspoon baking
powder

1 teaspoon grated lime
zest

1 teaspoon ground
cinnamon

1 cup sour cream

4 tablespoons butter
(½ stick), melted

Everybody loves a good homemade pound cake. It's rich and delicious.

1. Preheat the oven to 350°F. Spray a 9 by 5 by 3-inch loaf pan with non-stick cooking spray. Dust inside lightly with flour.

2. In a large bowl, cream the butter and sugar until smooth. Add the vanilla and eggs, one at a time, beating well after each addition. Combine the flour, baking powder, lime zest, and cinnamon. Add alternately with the sour cream, beating well after each addition. Pour the batter into the prepared pan. Bake for 55 to 60 minutes, until a toothpick inserted into the center of the cake comes out clean. Let cool for 15 minutes. Top the finished cake with the melted butter.

# Real Men Cook™ Gourmet Sweet Potato Pound Cake

## INGREDIENTS

1 cup milk

4 large eggs, at room temperature

4 tablespoons (½ stick) butter, melted

1 tablespoon vanilla extract

Two 16-ounce packages Real Men Cook Sweet Potato Pound Cake mix

¾ cup pecan pieces

¾ cup raisins

The sweet inspiration behind the Real Men Cook Sweet Potato Pound Cake can be found at Shakoor's Sweet Tooth. This Brooklyn, New York, bakery is located at 555 Troop Avenue, in the Bedford-Stuyvesant area of the city. There you'll find authentic sweet potato pound cake and a thriving gourmet bakery/restaurant owned by baker Shakoor Watson and his wife, Marissa. The Real Men Cook Sweet Potato Pound Cake may be purchased at a variety of Albertson's, Cubs, and Safeway grocery stores, or visit www.realmencook.com to order.

1. Preheat the oven to 350°F. Grease and flour a standard-size Bundt pan.

2. In a large mixing bowl, combine the milk, eggs, butter, and vanilla. Stir the wet ingredients into the cake mix and mix until smooth. Add the pecans and raisins.

3. Pour the batter into the prepared pan. Bake for 1 hour. To test for doneness, insert a toothpick into the cake until it comes out clean. Cool for 10 minutes and remove from the pan.

Serves 6 to 8

# Eugene Morris
# Chocolate Marble Cheesecake

## INGREDIENTS

### CRUST

1½ cups graham cracker crumbs

3 tablespoons sugar

3 tablespoons melted butter

3 tablespoons milk

1 ounce (1 square) semisweet chocolate, melted

### CHEESECAKE

Three 8-ounce packages cream cheese, at room temperature

1¾ cups sugar

3 tablespoons flour

½ teaspoon salt

5 eggs and 2 egg yolks

1 teaspoon vanilla extract

1 cup heavy cream

1 tablespoon sour cream

11 ounces unsweetened chocolate, melted

"Several men in my family cooked, and my family is in the restaurant business. The restaurant changed names and locations a few times—Papa's Inn became Orbitz. But it was solid, and I did just about every job imaginable—cooked short orders and waited tables, washed the dishes and took out the garbage.

"I enjoy cooking and I credit my parents. My dad could bake some serious biscuits; Mom cooked well too, but those biscuits . . . When I first moved out on my own, the first thing I wanted to learn was how to make those biscuits.

"One thing I discovered early on is that the ladies like to have men cook for them. So I learned how to burn on a budget, get a bottle of wine, make a decent meal, and not break the bank.

"I have three sisters, and all of us turned out to be really good cooks. I was truly blessed being around my family enjoying good food.

"Real Men Cook is therapeutic for me. In my business, running an advertising agency, I am running all the time, controlling stuff, keeping up with stuff, and it's always going in different directions. But when you bake, you can't rush it. You've got to slow down. I like to keep my focus on the presentation and watching my guests enjoy the meal.

"I love great food and the creative mastery that goes with it. Participating with Real Men Cook for over a decade is very special to me. So much so, I bought a bigger stove to make my signature dish for the event! But on the serious side, it gives me the opportunity to talk with the other men who share Father's Day with the thousands of people who attend. It's not just giving back; it's adding to the community and to the positive image of what Real Men can do."

1. Preheat the oven to 475°F.

2. Prepare the crust: Mix all of the crust ingredients together and press into the bottom of a 10-inch springform pan.

3. Using an electric mixer, beat the cream cheese until fluffy. Combine the sugar, flour, and salt and gradually add to the cheese, mixing until smooth; set aside.

4. In a separate bowl, mix the remaining ingredients together. Spoon the cheese batter and chocolate mixture alternately over the crust. Cut through the layers several times with a knife for a marbled effect.

5. Bake for 15 minutes. Reduce the temperature to 200°F and continue baking for 1 hour longer. Turn the oven off and let the cake rest with the door closed for 15 minutes. Let cool, chill, and serve.

Serves 8

**Eugene Morris is the president of E. Morris Communications. He has participated in more than twelve Real Men Cook events.**

## Fernando Jones
# Special Sweet Potato Pie

Fernando Jones

"Do this on Friday night 'round six, when the sun is easin' down.

"Put on your favorite blues CD, album, or tape. The more low-down, the better. The blues! Nothin' against jazz, R&B, or rock 'n' roll, but in order for this dish to act right, it's gotta be acclimated to the situation.

"The blues is like cooking from scratch. It's the same thing, taking what you've got and been left with and making something good-sounding and good for you. I'm from Mississippi, and ever since I was a little boy I watched my mother cook everything from scratch. Like corn bread, greens, and fish. Stews, cakes, and pies. Cooking from scratch and being from Mississippi go hand in hand, I guess.

"My grandmother passed away when my mother was very young, and the cooking duties for the family became hers, because she was a natural. The recipes from my mother are all basically from memory; nothing was written down. I got hooked on her pies, so I watched her

2 pounds sweet
potatoes, fresh or
canned

1 cup sugar

¼ pound (1 stick)
butter, melted

3 eggs, separated

1 tablespoon ground
cinnamon

Three 8-inch graham
cracker piecrusts

½ cup chopped pecans

'scratch out' those pies, peach, lemon, and apple, but especially those sweet potato pies.

"Now, I make a really, really nice and special sweet potato pie, which I feature at Real Men Cook. My special sweet potato pie has crushed pecans over the top and a graham cracker crust with just a little cinnamon on the bottom.

"When people come together, like friends, and family reunions, it's a very beautiful experience, and I plan to take part next year and forever. We are a brilliant and beautiful people, and if I wasn't black I would surely be trying to be black 'cause we can have some fun. This is like what I do at Christmas, cooking for nieces and nephews along with the rest of the family. Everything is positive and it's all about being treated like family."

1. Preheat the oven to 350°F.

2. Peel and boil the fresh potatoes until tender (or simmer the canned potatoes in a pot), then mash until potatoes are smooth. Place the potatoes into a mixing bowl, add the sugar, and stir in the melted butter. Add the egg yolks and stir.

3. Beat the egg whites with a whisk, until you have soft peaks. When you've mixed everything together, stir in the cinnamon and egg whites; the beaten egg whites give the pies a sheen.

4. Pour equal amounts of the potato filling into each pie crust; shake around gently until the filling is even and the crust is full. Bake for about 30 minutes. Check them at 20 minutes to make sure they're not cooking too fast.

5. When done, let cool for 10 minutes. Sprinkle on the pecan chips—press them in lightly. Set in the refrigerator and serve chilled.

Each pie serves about 6

Jay Williams

# Dr. Jay's Carmelitas

**INGREDIENTS**

CRUST

2 cups flour

1½ cups packed brown sugar

1 teaspoon baking soda

½ teaspoon salt

4 tablespoons (½ stick) butter or margarine

3 tablespoons flour

1 teaspoon vanilla extract

⅓ cup semisweet chocolate chips

⅓ cup peanut butter chips

⅓ cup butterscotch chips

⅓ cup white chocolate chips

½ cup macadamia nuts

One 12-ounce jar caramel ice cream topping

This dessert is sinfully delicious. Beware, they will go fast, so set some aside for yourself for later.

1. Preheat the oven to 350°F. Grease a 13 by 9-inch baking pan.

2. Prepare the crust: In a large mixing bowl, blend all of the crust ingredients until crumbly. Press 3 cups of the crust mixture onto the bottom of the baking pan and bake for 10 minutes.

3. Combine the flour, vanilla, all the chips, and the nuts in a bowl. When the crust is done, cover with the chip and nut mixture. Next, pour the caramel topping over the chips and nuts. Then, cover with the remaining crust mixture. Bake for 18 to 20 minutes, until golden brown. Let cool completely and cut into bars.

Makes about 10 to 12 bars

## Kevin Ashford

# Cool Coconut Pineapple Cheesecake

**INGREDIENTS**

¼ cup shredded coconut

2 eggs, separated

Two 8-ounce packages cream cheese, softened

½ teaspoon vanilla extract

½ cup sugar

½ cup crushed pineapple

1 graham cracker piecrust

This cheesecake will remind you of that exotic vacation, either the one you took on your honeymoon, or the one you're planning to take real soon. She will thank you for it.

1. Preheat the oven to 325°F.

2. Place half of the coconut in a skillet. Lightly toast the coconut over medium heat and set aside. Beat the egg whites to stiff peaks (do not overbeat) and set aside. In a separate mixing bowl, beat the cream cheese, vanilla, and sugar at medium speed until well blended. Add the egg yolks one at a time, beating for 1 minute after each addition. Fold in the egg whites, pineapple, and the remaining coconut. Mix well.

3. Pour the mixture into the crust and place on a cookie sheet. Bake for 25 minutes, or until the center is set. Turn the oven off and let the cake rest with the door closed for 5 to 10 minutes. Remove the cheesecake from the oven and let it cool on a wire rack.

4. Refrigerate the cheesecake for 2 hours and garnish with the toasted coconut before serving.

Serves 8

# CHAPTER SIX

# Life's Greatest Rewards

Children are life's greatest rewards. My children are my life. They are the beings that help make me the man and the father that I am.

Like any proud father, I will digress a moment to tell you just a little bit about my children . . .

The oldest, Angela, is married and living in Brooklyn, New York. Her preoccupation of the moment is caring for the second of the family's grandchildren. She is spending her new state of motherhood and domestication perfecting her grandmother Lydia's waffles.

Dr. Kweli, a recent graduate of Michigan State's School of Medicine, now a resident at Grant Memorial Hospital/Morehouse Medical College, in Atlanta, was finally able to escape the cold, mundane collegiate life in East Lansing, Michigan. Although a prodigious desire for the open road often led her to our door without much prior alert, Kweli is settling into the responsibilities that a career in child psychiatry requires. Still, I would never be surprised to get a familiar call from the road telling me she's " 'bout an hour away, what you cookin'?" in perfect ghettoese.

Ki-Afi Ra, an "Egyptologist" after only one trip to the Nile, lives mostly in airports rather than in an apartment. Formerly a buyer for several divisions of the Ford Motor Company, currently on an extended sabbatical, she is now in hot pursuit of any entrepreneurial venture that will lead her to a life of wealth, airplanes, boats, and trains, not at all unlike her Granny Lydia. From Atlanta or Washington, D.C., wherever she lands, I doubt that she will lose the unique ability to call home at the precise moment that food is being put on the table. It's like "smella-phone with an appetite."

Yosheyah is my oldest man-child. Since being away from home on the "college boy food plan," he has lost half of himself, suggesting as a reason that I ruined his taste for fast-food restaurants. He is a natural in the kitchen, enjoyed a short stint in catering, and is now living and working in Savannah.

Kilolo spent four years in rural mushroom-farming country in order to graduate from Lincoln University in Pennsylvania. A master's degree in math and history from Temple University and two years of teaching in Philadelphia's inner city have led to a new residency in Bear, Delaware, where in spite of her petite stature there lurks the appetite of a truck driver. Or perhaps a bear!

Gavriel, at an early age, could always be counted on to see his meals a second time. When we were traveling by auto or van, twenty minutes was usually his limit before demanding an emergency stop for him to eject semidigested meals. A graduate of Sullivan University in culinary science, he is part of the food service industry.

Kush, the youngest and most competitive eater, earned his

place at the table by being the fastest and least discriminating about his food choices. Conceived in Liberia, West Africa, and born in Cincinnati, no meal is complete for him without rice. Hormones and an addiction to hip-hop music have conspired to produce a less than stellar academic career to date, and we are not quite sure just what Kush will do with his life, but rest assured that rice will be present.

Rael, my bonus son and my wife's only non-bonus child, is a slowly recovering victim of being a much-loved, early, only child; first grandson; first great-grandson; his father's first child; and the focus of everyone's affection. Presently, he is learning how to eat "real" food and discovering a latent ability to "hook up" nutrition at home without restaurant takeouts, but for years he's devoured books much more frequently than a home-cooked meal, a skill achieved while earning a degree in chemistry at Florida A&M University.

Kevani Zelpah Moyo. Perhaps the most creative of our children, she, like her mother, Kimya, loved the performing arts. A dancer, scriptwriter, and video producer, at sixteen Zelpah was emerging from her childhood as a beautiful and engaging young woman, poised to enter Florida A&M University. As an honor student, cheerleader, and culturally conscious thought leader among her peers, Zelpah was destined to be a leader in whatever she chose to do. All of that ended on July 9, 1999, when a terrible car accident took Zelpah from us. Although we continue to mourn, we know her spirit is forever alive—especially on Father's Day.

So you can see, my kids are spread out. They live very busy lives, much like myself, but that's no excuse. I don't wait to hear from them; I pick up the phone and call. I don't need to talk with them every day, but they're on my mind 24/7. I am very much in their lives. I take my role as a father very seriously, and I would like to think that I am a major factor and force in their lives.

Sometimes I call them just to say hello or ask what's happening, and for those who need an extra boost or perhaps help to guide them to take that next step or "go to the next level," I am there, plane, train, car, or cell phone.

During Kwanza, my daughter Ki-Afi Ra asks all of her family and friends to come together and have an "intergenerational conversation piece." This dialogue allows for parents, grandparents, friends, and family to have their annual assessment of family growth. It is an eye-opening experience and one that I recommend for you to try. It is rewarding.

These recipes are big dishes to share with family and friends. Dr. Wayne Watson (Lemon Meringue Pie) loves to cook with his children, preparing recipes given to him by his mother. Greg Hardin's G.K.'s Wild Chili reminds us of our parents saying, "Here, taste this." Indeed, we love to taste them all. These dishes and time spent with the family are measures of love. Share these recipes with those you love and pass them down to the next generation.

## Bill Campbell

# Bill Campbell's Cajun/Creole "KYB"* Chops or Chicken!!!

### INGREDIENTS

Six 1-inch-thick loin pork chops, or 6 boneless, skinless chicken breasts (3 pounds)

3 tablespoons butter or virgin olive oil

1 large Spanish onion, chopped

4 garlic cloves, minced

1 teaspoon flour

2 teaspoons salt or salt substitute

2 teaspoons Dijon mustard

Black pepper, preferably freshly ground

Cayenne pepper, preferably freshly ground

1 tablespoon Matouk's Trinidadian Hot Sauce

7 drops Tabasco

3 drops Jamaican hellfire sauce

1 cup beef broth

2 tablespoons chopped dill or garlic dill pickle

1 lemon

Bill Campbell is the host and producer of ABC 7's *Chicagoing with Bill Campbell. Chicagoing* is a weekly program that showcases Chicago's rich history, the promise of its future, and the people, places, and possibilities of Chicago today. He also served as the station's director of community services. Bill has been a friend to Real Men Cook, both as a participant and pied piper, by assisting us in spreading the word throughout the community.

1. Remove the bones from the chops. Cut the chops in half sideways but *don't* split them entirely. Spread them out flat; this is called butterfly-ing. If you're using chicken breasts, pound them between sheets of plastic wrap to an equal thinness.

2. Heat 2 tablespoons of the butter in a skillet and brown the chops or chicken breasts on both sides; remove and set aside. Add the remaining tablespoon butter to the skillet, add the onion and garlic, and sauté for 3 to 5 minutes. Add the flour, salt, mustard, black and cayenne pepper to taste, the Matouk's, Tabasco, and hellfire sauce, and stir until blended. Heat the beef broth, then slowly add it and the pickle to the skillet; simmer for 7 minutes.

3. Return the chops or chicken to the skillet and slather the sauce over them. Cover and let simmer until tender, about 15 minutes. Right before serving, squeeze lemon juice over the dish. Enjoy! Have lots of ice water handy!!!!!!!

Serves 6

* "KYB" = "kicks your butt!"

Cliff Rome

# Pan-Seared Atlantic Salmon
# with Vodka-Dill Cream Sauce

**INGREDIENTS**

1 tablespoon olive oil

1 teaspoon chopped
shallot

1 teaspoon chopped
garlic

2 cups chicken broth

1 cup heavy cream

1 tablespoon fresh dill

Salt and black pepper

6 ounces bow tie pasta

2 salmon fillets
(1 pound)

1 cup chopped tomato

⅓ cup vodka

Salmon is an important food in the Native American diet, high in protein, and rich in vitamins A and B and in omega-3 oils. Salmon migrate from salt water to spawn in fresh water. The Atlantic salmon is just one of many varieties of North American salmon.

1. Heat a saucepot for 2 minutes over medium-low heat. Add the olive oil, shallot, and garlic and sauté for 2 minutes. Add the broth and cook until the volume is reduced by half. Add the heavy cream and cook for 3 minutes. Remove from the heat; add the dill and salt and pepper to taste.

2. Cook the pasta according to package directions; drain.

3. Spray a skillet with nonstick cooking spray or use a little olive oil. Heat the skillet for 2 minutes over medium heat. Season the salmon with salt and pepper. Cook, skin side down, for 2 to 3 minutes; turn and cook for 2 to 3 minutes.

4. Add the tomato and vodka to the dill-cream sauce; cook over low heat for 5 minutes. Fold in the pasta and cook for 3 minutes. Place the pasta in a serving dish and put the salmon on top.

Serves 1 or 2

# Contributed by Curlee Adams

## If I Should Die Tomorrow: A Black Man to His Son

Author Unknown

Listen, son, while we have this time together
Let's not spend it just talking about the weather
There are black men who are dying every single day
From every cause and in every kind of way

Many have died in wars in which nobody has won
Many have died in the streets from some policeman's gun
But the saddest thing of all that is so hard to understand
Most of them are killed by some other young black man

So while I have you close, while I have you near
There are things I must say, things you must hear
'Cause far too often people fail to communicate
What they wished to say many times comes much too late

For a black man this world will always be a struggle
For anyone, for that matter, but for you it will be double
But never think for a moment you cannot conquer anything
Always remember your people were once kings and queens

And although you live in this country called America
Your spirit is from the motherland, continent of Africa
And though you love to emulate your idol Michael Jordan
Remember your ancestors drank from the River Jordan

Many times you've asked me, Dad, why all the history
'Cause where we're at now, son, is not where we should be
There is something that is just so terribly wrong
It's like the black man is lost in a twilight zone

When you see young brothers not much older than you
Killing each other like there's just nothing else to do
Over materialism, a misguided statement, an ounce of crack
I don't want you to think it's always been like that

When you see black men on corners holding up the walls
Remember the time black men stood so tall
All that wasted talent, they should be busy creating—
Don't they know their skills are needed? The world is waiting

There's so many inventions that are kept hid
Not to mention the great wonders of the pyramids
For instance, who do you think is the father of medicine
There's even speculation about the inventions of Edison

When you see black women walking up and down streets
Jumping in and out of cars for some trick or treat
Remember it's only because they have lost their place
But it's a direct result of their man's fall from grace

And as you grow up being black, proud and strong
It's incumbent on you to try to uplift your own
If you meet a sister and your heart goes to thumping
It's incumbent on you to respect that black woman

'Cause among all the colors of this universal equation
The world hates to admit it, she's the mother of creation
Will it be your generation who puts her back on her throne?
Will it be your generation who'll correct these wrongs?

So, son, as you meet this world with all its problems to bear
Remember Langston said, "Life for me ain't been no crystal stair"
And if I should die tomorrow by any stroke of fate
I'm glad we had this talk before it was too late.

## Curlee Adams

# Curlee Adams's Vegetable Casserole

**INGREDIENTS**

5 pounds frozen California blend vegetables

Two 10¾-ounce cans condensed cream of broccoli and cheese soup

1 pound Cheddar cheese, shredded

One 15-ounce can bread crumbs

1. Preheat the oven to 350°F. Butter a 12 by 8-inch baking dish.

2. Steam the vegetables for 15 minutes and place in the baking dish. Heat the soup and pour on top of the vegetables. Sprinkle the cheese on top along with the bread crumbs. Bake for 40 to 45 minutes.

Serves 12 to 14

Curlee Adams and his son, Malachi

## Don Jackson

# Chicken Breasts in Tomato Sauce

Don Jackson

**INGREDIENTS**

2 pounds mushrooms, sliced

3 tablespoons vegetable oil

6 large onions, diced

4 garlic cloves, chopped

3 large green bell peppers, diced

Eight 12-ounce cans tomato sauce

Eight 12-ounce cans stewed tomatoes

2 teaspoons salt

2 teaspoons black pepper

¼ cup honey

1 cup dry white wine

10 pounds boneless, skinless chicken breasts

3 tablespoons grated sharp Cheddar cheese

Tomatoes are the key ingredient in this dish. This fruit is better recognized as a vegetable. Medical reports show that tomatoes are a great source of vitamins A, B, and C, and potassium, iron, and phosphorus. They are also high in lycopene, a carotenoid we get mainly from eating tomato products; studies show lycopene helps in preventing prostate cancer. Real Men Cook is dedicated to informing the community about prostate cancer, one of the leading causes of death in African American men in this country. Real Men Cook has taken on this cause by providing prostate cancer testing in Chicago.

For more information on prostate cancer in the African American community, check with your doctor and visit our website, www.real mencook.com.

1. Preheat the oven to 350°F.

2. In a large skillet, sauté the mushrooms in the vegetable oil. Add the onions, garlic, and green peppers and sauté until soft and brown. Add the tomato sauce and stir; add the stewed tomatoes, salt, and pepper. Add the honey and wine; stir and let simmer for 15 minutes.

3. Arrange the chicken breasts side by side in a large aluminum roasting pan. Pour the tomato mixture over them. Cover with aluminum foil and bake for 50 minutes to 1 hour. Remove the foil from the baking dish and sprinkle the cheese over the chicken and tomato sauce. Put the baking dish back into the oven without the aluminum foil and bake another 10 minutes, or until the cheese is completely melted.

Serves 50

**Don Jackson is president of Central City Productions, the largest African American–owned television production company in the Windy City. He participated in the first Real Men Cook event in 1990 at the Museum of Science and Industry.**

Mike Bruton's Creole
Seafood and Chicken
Gumbo *(page 127)*

James Battiste's
Fried Chicken *(page 30)*

Anthony Glover's Sweet
and Sour Teriyaki Chicken
*(page 71)*

Lafayette Ford's
La La's Chicken Curry
*(page 152)*

Jimmy's T's "On-Time" Bar-b-que Meats (*page 146*) and Earl Calloway's Deadline Potato Salad (*page 55*)

Arthur E. Teele's Miami
Conch Fritters *(page 7)*
and Greg T. Hinton's
Sautéed Crab Cakes
with Shrimp or Lobster
*(page 56)*

Howard Hill's International
Turkey Chili *(page 29)*

Dr. Cliff West's Seafood Paella
*(page 54)* and Chef "Sweet"
Basil Brathwaite's Rum Punch
*(page 74)*

Cliff Rome's Pan-Seared Atlantic
Salmon with Vodka-Dill Cream Sauce
*(page 114)*

Earl Carter's and Ray Blackburns's Chicken Breast Piccata and Golden Rice *(page 114)*

Leonard Thomas's Cool Hens in Jamaica *(page 155)*

Andrew J. Williams's
Braised Beef Tenderloin
*(page 6)*

Tommy Conley's
Beef Pie *(page 132)*

Kevin Ashford's Row da Boat Curry Pineapple Shrimp *(page 154)*

Ira Wilson's Seafood Viola: Shrimp and Crawfish Etoufée *(page 60)*

Lorenzo E. Martin's Sour
Cream Gingerbread
*(page 36)*

Terrence Davis's
Creamy Pecan Pralines
*(page 86)*

Chef Michael Johnson's
Sour Cream Pound
Cake *(page 101)*

Avell Collier's Bread
Puddin' *(page 98)*

John Russell's
Apple Peach
Cobbler *(page 31)*

Chef Michael Seay's Famous
Flourless Chocolate Cake
*(page 99)*

Charles Sherrell's Don't Be a Boar Feast *(page 72)*

## Dr. Wayne Watson
# Lemon Meringue Pie

Dr. Wayne Watson

**INGREDIENTS**

One 9-inch piecrust

2 cups sugar

3 tablespoons cornstarch

3 egg yolks, lightly beaten

Grated zest of 1 lemon

¼ cup fresh lemon juice

1 tablespoon butter or margarine

4 egg whites

1 teaspoon vanilla extract

"My work keeps me on the go a lot, so I don't get a chance to cook as much as I would like to. To me cooking is an art. Before you get to the spiritual level, think about the aroma it gives to the house. It makes a house a home. I love cooking and sharing with my kids—and holidays are extra special in my family. This is also the time where I measure the growth and direction of my kids. When you get all the kids in the kitchen cooking, it's all laughs from when you start until you finish. And when you think back to what we're laughing about, I don't know, it's just the overall feeling that it's a lot of laughs, a lot of fun, and a lot of enjoyment. There's a lot of signifying, too, me sitting back watching the kids interact with each other now. It's a time to assess and measure them.

"Everything I learned about food, I learned from my mother. I cook from her recipes to this day. I can cook anything from paella to soul food to a stuffed chicken with orange honey glaze sauce roasted inside of a brown bag—the entire gamut, hands down. I love to bake cakes, but I really enjoy baking pies. If I bake an apple pie, you'll taste a bit of me in it because my apple pie is going to have just a bit of tartness. You know it's sweet but a little tart too. I'm a nice person, but I'm a little sharp at times—have a cutting edge.

"Real Men Cook is important to me because it's a unique experience. I like the whole concept of bringing black men together on Father's Day. . . . the camaraderie, men doing something together in a positive way. I like that entire concept . . . and that's why I did it. I still believe that it is a very positive concept that is being put forth."

1. Preheat the oven to 400 °F. Prick the bottom of the piecrust with a fork several times. Bake the piecrust for 10 minutes, or until brown. Cool for 5 minutes.

2. Stir together 1 cup of the sugar and the cornstarch in a 3-quart saucepan. Gradually stir in 1¼ cups cold water until smooth. Add the egg yolks, stirring constantly. Bring to a boil over medium heat and let boil for 1 minute, then remove from the heat. Stir in the lemon zest,

lemon juice, and butter. Cover with waxed paper and cook for about 5 minutes over medium-low heat, stirring two or three times. Cool in the refrigerator for 30 minutes. Pour the filling into the piecrust.

3. Beat the egg whites until frothy, until they foam. Add the vanilla, and gradually add the remaining cup of sugar. Beat until soft peaks form. Continue beating until stiff peaks form. Spread over the cooled pie. Put in the oven for 10 minutes, until the meringue has browned a little.

Serves 6 to 8

**Dr. Wayne Watson is the chancellor of the City Colleges of Chicago. He is ageless, the father of three, and a grandfather.**

## Greg DeShields
# Fried Chicken Salad

Greg DeShields

**INGREDIENTS**

1 pound boneless,
skinless chicken breasts

½ cup flour

2 tablespoons hot sauce

1 teaspoon seasoned
salt

½ teaspoon garlic
powder

¼ teaspoon black
pepper

1 cup vegetable oil

¼ pound mixed salad
greens

2 tablespoons ranch
dressing

This is a new take on an old recipe. It isn't your mother's chicken salad. This well-seasoned spicy version is refreshing and different. It combines a good old southern fried chicken technique with a light twist, adding mixed field greens, creating a new and enigmatic dish. Share this one at your next family picnic.

1. Cut the chicken into bite-size pieces. Combine the flour, 2 tablespoons water, the hot sauce, seasoned salt, garlic powder, and pepper. Coat the chicken pieces in the mixture.

2. Heat the vegetable oil in a medium frying pan over medium heat until hot. Fry the chicken pieces until golden brown. Toss the mixed greens together with the fried chicken pieces. Top with ranch dressing.

Serves 2 to 4

## Greg Hardin

# G.K.'s Wild Chili

Greg Hardin

**H**aving my sons, Bradley and Gregory, and my granddaughter, Heaven, in my life is the best Father's Day gift for me. As a father, I share many things with my children, including the number one quote: "Be the best at anything you do in life." This was taught to me by my grandmother, Susie Jones.

*As a father I must share the wisdom*
*As a father I must share the knowledge*
*As a father I must show tough love. It may hurt but . . .*
*As a father I must share the reasons . . .*
*As a father I must share the fact of becoming a bright young, strong, helpful,*
    *loving black individual*
*As a father I must show the love of a real black man*

### INGREDIENTS

Two 28-ounce cans
Brooks hot kidney
beans

One 28-ounce can
stewed tomatoes

1 cup diced onion

1 pound ground turkey

1 tablespoon chili
powder

One 1¼-ounce package
chili seasoning mix

¼ teaspoon crushed red
pepper flakes

⅛ teaspoon cayenne
pepper

(Six cans of beer)

1. Place the kidney beans in a large pot. Add the tomatoes, onion, and 1 cup water. Let simmer for 20 minutes over medium-low heat. (Take a beer break.)

2. Place the ground turkey into a skillet. Brown with a pinch of the chili powder.

3. Add the chili mix and the remaining chili powder to the bean mixture. Add the red pepper flakes and cayenne. When the turkey is browned, add it to the chili and simmer for 30 minutes. (Now it's time to take a seat and eat. Take another beer break and enjoy.)

Serves 4 to 6

Ibn Sharrieff

# Shrimp and Vegetable Linguine

### INGREDIENTS

½ cup sliced carrots

½ cup broccoli florets

½ pound linguine

4 tablespoons (½ stick) butter

3 garlic cloves, chopped

1 pound large shrimp, peeled and deveined

½ cup bread crumbs

1 cup white wine (semidry)

1 tablespoon chopped fresh parsley

Salt and black pepper

In memoriam, to a brother who was well loved and respected.

1. Bring 4 cups water to a boil in a saucepan; add the carrots and broccoli. Cook for 5 to 7 minutes, until fork tender; drain and set aside.

2. Cook the linguine according to package directions; drain and set aside.

3. In a skillet, melt the butter over low heat and add the garlic. Sauté for 1 minute. Add the shrimp and sauté for 5 minutes, or until the shrimp turn pink. Add the bread crumbs and continue to sauté the mixture. Add the wine and sauté another 5 minutes. Toss in the cooked vegetables. Add the parsley, and salt and pepper to taste. Serve over the linguine.

Serves 2

James Clark

# Jay Cee's Nautical Nectar Salad

INGREDIENTS

1 cup mayonnaise

¼ cup finely chopped onion

½ cup finely chopped celery

½ cup finely chopped green bell pepper

½ teaspoon garlic powder

½ teaspoon paprika

½ teaspoon seasoned salt

½ pound cooked crabmeat

½ pound cooked small salad shrimp

½ pound cooked lobster meat

One 7½-ounce can red sockeye salmon

1 pound small pasta shells, cooked, drained, and cooled

This seafood salad is light and easy, perfect for a hot summer night dinner. Serve it with crackers and fresh fruit.

In a large bowl, whisk the mayonnaise until smooth. Add the onion, celery, green pepper, garlic powder, paprika, and seasoned salt. Mix well and fold in the crabmeat, shrimp, lobster, and salmon. Add the pasta shells and continue to mix gently until well combined. Cover and refrigerate for about 3 hours before serving.

Serves 4 to 6

1 tablespoon olive oil

1 tablespoon dry red wine

2 tablespoons liquid smoke

2 tablespoons teriyaki sauce with pineapple juice

2 tablespoons Worcestershire sauce

Four 12-ounce top sirloin steaks (or substitute four 24-ounce prime porterhouse steaks)

SEASONING RUB:

1 tablespoon Mrs. Dash Natural Seasoning

1 tablespoon garlic powder

1 tablespoon Lawry's seasoned salt

1 tablespoon lemon-pepper seasoning

1 tablespoon barbecue seasoning

1 tablespoon hickory seasoning

1 tablespoon Accent

1 tablespoon Adolph's meat tenderizer

1 tablespoon minced onion

1 tablespoon minced garlic

2 tablespoons melted butter

# Keith Rozier
# Steppin' Char-Grilled Steaks

When it comes to grilling, men have their own techniques that give them bragging rites, a ritual that has been passed down from generation to generation. This recipe will give you bragging rites, too.

1. Combine the olive oil, wine, liquid smoke, teriyaki sauce, and Worcestershire sauce. Coat both sides of the steaks with the mixture.

2. Combine all of the ingredients for the rub and apply to both sides of the steaks.

3. Prepare the grill for indirect grilling: the charcoal should be directed to both sides of your grill. Add presoaked hardwood to red-hot charcoal for smoking and smoke flavor. (Tip: Presoak your favorite wood, such as mesquite or hickory, with ½ cup red wine.)

4. Oil the grill; be careful not to spray oil directly onto the grill while coals are blazing. Place the steaks in the center of the grill. Place the lid on the grill. Cook the steaks for 15 minutes on each side (depending upon thickness of the steak and the degree of desired doneness). Keep the lid closed during the cooking, as it seals in the smoky flavor. Baste the steaks once on each side with melted butter. Remove the steaks from the grill and serve immediately.

Serves 4

## Leonard Kaigler

# Shrimp Soup

INGREDIENTS

Three 10¾-ounce cans condensed cream of mushroom soup

One 10¾-ounce can condensed tomato soup

1½ pounds medium shrimp, peeled and deveined

1 cup diced onion

After a long hard day, this is a quick and easy dish to make. The more shrimp, the better! If you like, add some sautéed fresh mushrooms and garnish with chopped parsley. You may substitute white wine for the water. Serve it over jasmine rice for a nutty and fragrant taste. It is *delicious!*

1. In a large saucepan, combine the mushroom soup, tomato soup, and 3 cups water (for a creamier soup, substitute milk for the water). Bring to a boil, reduce the heat, and let simmer, stirring frequently.

2. In a skillet, sauté the shrimp and onion for about 2 minutes, or until the shrimp turns pink. Drain and add to the soup. Simmer for about 10 minutes. Serve the soup over rice: a great southern dish.

Serves 6 to 8

## Mike Bruton

# Creole Seafood and Chicken Gumbo

**INGREDIENTS**

6 tablespoons roux

1 tablespoon black pepper

1 tablespoon gumbo filé

1 tablespoon cayenne pepper

2 teaspoons salt

3 tablespoons Tony Chachere's Creole Seasoning

1 chicken (2½ to 3 pounds), cut up into serving pieces

1 pound andouille sausage, cut into ¼-inch slices

4 stalks celery, chopped

1 medium onion, chopped

2 cups chopped green onions (green and white parts)

1 cup chopped fresh parsley

1 pound large shrimp, peeled and deveined

2 pounds lump crabmeat (6 to 8 whole blue crabs, cleaned, if available)

Gumbo is one of the mainstays of Creole cuisine. The key to a good gumbo begins with a thick dark roux. This is the base that gives this dish its rich flavor. Many recipes use either okra or filé powder to thicken the stew. Filé powder is made from the ground, dried leaves of the sassafras tree. Many families keep their gumbo recipe a secret. Thanks for sharing this recipe with us, Mike.

1. In a large pot, bring 2 quarts water to a boil while adding the roux, black pepper, gumbo filé, cayenne, salt, and Creole seasoning. When the roux is dissolved, reduce the heat to medium; this should take no more than 30 minutes. Stir constantly, so that it's thoroughly mixed.

2. Add the chicken and cook for 40 minutes, then add the sausage, celery, onion, and green onions. Continue cooking for 20 to 30 minutes, then add the parsley, shrimp, and crabmeat. Simmer until shrimp and crabmeat are cooked through, about 5 minutes. Serve with rice.

Serves 10 to 12

## Monroe Anderson

# Monroe's Mean, Lean Greens

### INGREDIENTS

1 smoked turkey wing

5 pounds mixed fresh mustard and collard greens

2 tablespoons bacon fat

1 large Vidalia onion, finely chopped

6 cups chicken broth (preferably homemade)

Juice of 1 small lemon

3 garlic cloves, minced

2 tablespoons sea salt

2 tablespoons light brown sugar

2 tablespoons red wine vinegar

2 tablespoons Worcestershire sauce

1 teaspoon crushed red pepper flakes

Dash of Louisiana hot sauce

"I started experimenting with cooking as a teenager because I had very selective taste buds and didn't like what most folks cooked—even my momma.

"I've been cooking since, although, in reality, I'm a weekend cook. I frequently cook large quantities of chili, greens, black-eyed peas, pinto beans, red beans, or gumbo and freeze much of it in small containers for meals later in the week or month.

"I usually look at several recipes from cookbooks and online, then figure out what I want to keep and what I don't want to use. From there, the gut feelings and the artistry take over."

1. Boil the smoked turkey wing until tender enough so that the meat can be pulled off the bone with a fork. Discard the skin.

2. Clean the greens: remove the grit by washing in the kitchen sink several times. Cut the leaves into 3-inch diagonal strips with a sharp knife.

3. Heat the bacon fat in a large skillet and sauté the onion until soft and translucent.

4. Put the broth into a large kettle. Add the sautéed onion. Add the lemon juice, garlic, salt, sugar, vinegar, Worcestershire sauce, red pepper flakes, and hot sauce. Add the greens and smoked turkey meat.

5. Bring to a boil, lower the heat, and let simmer for 45 minutes.

Serves 4

**Monroe Anderson is the editor of *Savoy* magazine, in Chicago. He is married with two children.**

# Reggie Carter
# Seafood-Stuffed Green Peppers

**INGREDIENTS**

6 medium green bell
peppers

2 pounds medium
shrimp, peeled and
deveined

6 ounces crabmeat

1½ cups cooked rice

½ cup chopped celery

½ cup chopped onion

2 tablespoons chopped
pimento

¾ cup mayonnaise

1 teaspoon curry
powder

½ teaspoon salt

Black pepper

½ cup bread crumbs

Butter or margarine

"I was raised in New Orleans, back in the bayou. I learned to cook from my mother and stepfather, who was a cook in the Navy. He enjoyed cooking rabbit, gumbo, and chili, and my mother enjoyed cooking Creole dishes. To me, cooking is a lot of fun, and I like to see people eat good food and be happy, especially my wife and son. I try to cook at least three times a week, keeping with my family tradition of preparing Creole and Cajun dishes, including jambalaya, red beans and rice, and my favorite, shrimp Creole.

"Before moving to Chicago, I was a short-order cook back in New Orleans for a sandwich shop called Pack-a-Jug. There, I cooked hamburgers, hot sausages, fried chicken, and shrimp.

"Once I arrived in Chicago, I hooked up with my natural father. Discovering that he did a lot of cooking also, we would do some things together, including some catering. My dad is a good cook, but I think I outshine him in my favorites.

"When I really need some special ingredient that I can't find in Chicago, I call my mother and she would send it to me.

"Real Men Cook is a great event, and it's a lot of fun. You get a chance to meet a lot of people, and when we regroup and meet again the next year, it gets better and better. I have to credit and thank Real Men Cook, because it got my father and me started in catering, and I do some outside festivals. After Real Men Cook is over, people recognize me as the guy who cooks shrimp Creole. That's a real good feeling when people look for you and they know that you have good-quality food."

1. Preheat the oven to 350°F.

2. Cut off the top of each green pepper; remove the seeds and membranes. Bring salted water to a boil in a 3-quart saucepan, place the peppers in the water, and cook for 5 minutes; drain well and set aside.

3. Combine the shrimp, crabmeat, rice, celery, onion, and pimento in a large bowl. Add the mayonnaise, curry powder, salt, and pepper to taste,

and mix thoroughly. Stuff the peppers with the seafood mixture. Sprinkle each pepper with bread crumbs and dot with butter.

4. Place the stuffed peppers in a 1½-quart baking dish. Place the baking dish in a larger baking pan and pour in ½ inch of hot water. Bake for 30 minutes.

Serves 6

## William N. Reynolds
# North African Chicken Stew

### INGREDIENTS

½ cup olive oil

4 pounds chicken thighs

½ pound onions, diced

5 garlic cloves, chopped

2 tablespoons chopped fresh ginger

4 tablespoons ground cumin

1 tablespoon ground turmeric

1 teaspoon ground coriander

½ teaspoon grated nutmeg

½ teaspoon saffron threads (optional)

¼ teaspoon ground cloves

2 bay leaves

Bill Reynolds is committed to the field of culinary education and has always been a friend and key consultant to Real Men Cook. He is a man who knows how to get it done, whatever it is and whenever it is scheduled. He is also a mastermind at creating a community resource. He is developing an institutional outreach facility through the City Colleges of Chicago under the direction of Chicago City College chancellor and Real Men Cook volunteer Dr. Wayne Watson. Bill is the director of a $6 million building at the Chicago Park District's South Shore Cultural Center, an interim location while the new Washburne Culinary Institute is being built. This South Shore facility will remain a part of the Chicago Park District. Having this program at the center is a historic collaboration between the city agencies that will serve the interest of a large community on the rise.

William N. Reynolds

6 cups chicken broth

1 pound carrots, peeled and cut into 1-inch pieces

½ pound yellow turnips (rutabagas), peeled and cut into 1-inch pieces

½ pound sweet potatoes, peeled and diced large

½ pound zucchini, cut into ¼-inch slices

½ pound green bell peppers, cut into 1-inch pieces

2 medium tomatoes, cut into quarters

1 chili pepper, seeded and diced

1 cup cooked chickpeas (also known as garbanzo beans)

2 tablespoons cornstarch mixed in ½ cup *cold* water

COUSCOUS:

1 pound couscous

1 cup sliced almonds, toasted

1 cup raisins, plumped in 1 cup boiling water

1 cup chopped fresh parsley

1. Preheat a heavy deep pot (or Dutch oven) over medium-high heat. Add the olive oil and brown the chicken on both sides. Add the onions and garlic and sauté until the onion is translucent, approximately 5 minutes. Reduce the heat to medium and add the remaining spices and the chicken broth. Let simmer for 30 minutes.

2. Add the carrots, turnips, and sweet potatoes to the stew and continue to simmer for 15 minutes. Add the zucchini, peppers, tomatoes, chili, chickpeas, and cornstarch mixture and cook an additional 15 minutes, bringing the stew to a boil. Let boil for 5 minutes, then reduce the heat and simmer for 10 minutes.

3. While the stew is boiling, prepare the couscous according to package directions. Mix in the almonds, raisins, and parsley.

4. Plate the stew, beginning with a mound of couscous in the middle of a deep-sided platter and serve the stew around the perimeter, or serve the stew and couscous separately in two bowls or casserole dishes.

Serves 8

## Tommy Conley
# Tommy's Beef Pie

### INGREDIENTS

1 pound lean ground beef

2 cups seasoned croutons

One 8-ounce can tomato sauce

2 teaspoons instant minced onion

½ teaspoon salt

2 eggs, beaten

½ cup sliced fresh or canned mushrooms, drained if canned

¾ cup chopped green bell pepper

1 cup shredded Cheddar cheese

1 medium tomato, cut into ½-inch slices

In memory of 1999 Real Men Cook participant Tommy Conley. He will truly be missed.

This is a Real Men Cook recipe. It's great on a cold and blustery winter's day. Serve with a side salad.

1. Preheat the oven to 375°F.

2. Combine the beef, 1 cup of the croutons, the tomato sauce, onion, salt, and 1 egg. Press onto the sides and bottom of a 9-inch pie plate. Mix ½ cup of the croutons, 1 egg, the mushrooms, green pepper, and cheese; spread on top of the meat mixture. Arrange the tomato slices and remaining ½ cup croutons on top. Bake for about 25 minutes.

Serves 6

# CHAPTER SEVEN

# A Family of Men

P roducing an event of the magnitude of Real Men Cook is a daunting task, even though it is a task imbued with love. I suppose I should start at the beginning and tell you how RMC came into existence in the first place.

RMC actually started off in another form. A woman named Lana Turner founded and was producing an annual event in New York City called "Men Who Cook." It featured men cooking and serving their favorite dishes to an upscale audience. Thanks to a friend, Michael Scott, who at the time was director of Special Events for the City of Chicago, Lana was introduced to my wife. The event was already successful in its home market, and Ms. Turner seemed to welcome our call expressing interest in expanding it to Chicago, considering that she was aware of others who had copied her model without acknowledgment. In spite of being interested in working with us, it became very clear early on that Ms. Turner was fully occupied by the scope of her responsibilities in New York. She suggested that we proceed without her, which we did, christening our newly constituted event

"Real Men Cook for Charity" to distinguish it from the New York model.

As with most ambitious ventures, we wanted ours to be bigger and better. Armed with our new name, we set about the task of building an event in Chicago that could ultimately be exported nationwide. With some tweaks and turns, we quickly accomplished what we set out to do and wisely made Father's Day the focal point. Our event now proudly claims impact in fifteen major cities, including Atlanta, Dallas, Detroit, Miami, Houston, Los Angeles, New Orleans, New York, Philadelphia, and Washington, D.C. It is now the largest recognized national urban Father's Day event in the country.

The men we wanted to be involved in the event were to be both single and married. They would work in various capacities and reflect the diversity of involvement and thought that make up the absolute best of what the African American community has to offer. Collectively, they would represent the fundamental positive values of black family life. In order to find these men and get them to participate, we turned to a group of women from various professional backgrounds. They reached out into the community in their various fields of interest and reeled in men of exception and note who believed in our principles.

Planning for RMC begins in late October or early November, long before the actual event day, which occurs simultaneously in fifteen different cities. We make presentations to potential sponsors and select sites. Each event also starts with a series of social affairs designed to expose invited males to the history and operational aspects of RMC. The organizing team in each city uses these social affairs to provide participants with background information, photos, and film from previous events and round-robin introductions to the men who have signed on for participation. Generally, these sessions turn into highly social occasions with the men bragging about the what and how of the cooking they do.

Planning intensifies in February and March. When the hallowed traditions of Mother's Day have been celebrated, our coordinators and volunteers, many of whom are mothers themselves, begin the rollout of preparations that have been taking place for the previous six months. They are the ones to light a fire under the men, as it were. There is a rush of recruitment rallies, recipes are accumulated for the annual cookbook, and there are also certification classes, developed to meet the requirements of various boards of health. These classes are essential to ensure that proper cooking techniques, food-holding temperatures, and sanitary serving standards are adhered to. At the rallies, there is more bragging; evaluation of who's "throwing down," whose "rep" is in danger as a result of the past year's performance; sizing up the neophytes; and verbal jousting matches about whose line will be the longest. There are also other jibes, especially among the single men, about who will be doing the most "pullin' "—of sisters, that is—drawn from the largely female audience who come out to see these Real Men cook. There is a lot of "lyin' and signifyin'" about who can and who can't and then, presto, it's time to put on a "game face" and go.

Getting ready is a serious thing for any brother taking part in this effort. Unless he is a food service professional, cooking even sample-sized portions for three hundred to four hundred people takes concentrated effort. The final countdown begins during Memorial Day weekend. For those who plan to smoke, grill, or deep-fry their RMC dishes, it is time to locate grills; clean, tighten, or replace parts lost in the basement or garage; and, in the process, undertake long-overdue cleanouts of necessary cooking paraphernalia. An inventory of items needed for the big day usually requires a trip to a local home repair center or cooking supply store. I'll bet that the Home Depots, Loweses, Crate & Barrels, and Williams Sonomas of the world see an appreciable jump in sales as preparation for RMC goes into hot-and-heavy mode.

And so, Father's Day arrives. Tables and chairs are being set up by volunteers looking forward to the end of an exhausting day. The sponsors' area, children's workshop, health screening area, the stage, the broadcast area where the live remote will carry the message to the listening community—all are made ready. The earliest arrivals are generally men who will be cooking outside. They man smokers, grills, and deep fryers for the fried turkeys that have begun to invade the tradition of roasting for holiday seasons.

At 2:00 P.M. an African drum call signals the opening ceremony. From the stage, we are encouraged to all come together, taking a silent moment to remember the Real Men in our lives: the fathers, coaches, uncles, grandfathers, older men, and friends who have made a difference for us. The opening ritual is punctuated by the drum call and the pouring of a libation honoring ancestors and recently departed men. There is an acknowledgment of the volunteers, sponsors, and special guests, and then there is a roll call where each man calls out his name and years of participation.

Some of these men are accomplished, gifted, and well trained. Some have actually learned to be more adept at the kitchen ritual just to join the ranks of the brothers. Many remember their fathers and simply want to do something meaningful in their honor. Some have not had the benefit of having Dad at home during their life but are committed to forging a new family legacy of fatherhood for their own children. Many cook and serve with their sons and daughters at their sides.

At 3:00 the doors open for those families and friends, some of whom have been waiting for as much as an hour. They are in line now, hungry, happy, and in anticipation of the best three-hour food sampling of the year. Thousands of eager attendees seek out their favorite "Sunday chef" or just fall into one of the many lines forming with people straining to see what is being featured here or there. An amazing blend of production lines are serving sample-sized portions—just enough for a taste. The interaction between the men and the crowd becomes a love ritual. Attendees ask for more or a larger piece—"Come on, Dad!"—sometimes selecting the piece they want based on size or location—"just a corner piece." They are generally admonished, "If you want more, you have to get back in line so others can be served." You see smiles lighting up their faces or else frowns of faux intimidation—whatever it takes to get another taste. Attention shifts suddenly at the announcement "Hey, girl, he's got shrimp over there!" Nurturing mothers and fathers line up with their children. Familiar deejay music wafts through the air. Bowls and plates are overflowing. Volunteers scurry around searching for more napkins, forks, and bowls. Charcoal is sought as salsa is being served. All is accompanied by dancing to live music.

"Somebody said there are hot yeast rolls inside!"

"Did you get some of that gumbo? There's a brother from N'awlins over there in the corner spot."

"Momma, can I have seconds?"

"Hey, brother, happy Father's Day!"

"You know, my brother can really cook—he should be doing this!"

"Did you find the peach cobbler?"

"My God, look at those turkey legs!"

"Hey, where can I buy one of those aprons for my dad?"

Black cowboys and cowgirls demonstrate and give pony rides to the kids while clowns and painters decorate little faces with cat whiskers and spiders. Toy train rides, inflatable jungle gyms, chess games, and staged entertainment . . . giant balloons fill as the crowd swells. Bellies are becoming full and fulfilled. Along one side, there is health screening for heart and prostate. In line with our mission to build families and save lives, these are sponsored areas with information to improve family well-being.

Weeks, days, and now hours of preparation are coming to an end. It's Father's Day. Men, some out of food already, are helping others. High fives are thrown up with boasts of whose line was the longest, who was left standing, what group of sisters came back for more. Men are embracing, sharing plans for and knowing better now what to do next year. Everyone is happily exhausted. Those three hours have seemed like forever—so much energy compressed into so little time.

And then, it is over.

Cleaning up and packing to leave, brothers take a moment to sit on ice chests, sharing a cold one or a punch with an island twist. They hug babies and wives. Sweat-soaked helpers are looking for anyone who might have anything left. Any significant amount of food that is left over is being prepared to take to the homeless. Good luck! Most of the pots have been picked clean.

Long shadows and fatigue end the day's expressions of love. Thousands reluctantly leave the grounds, some pausing to offer help with the cleanup. Many just want to stop to say thank you to these Real Men who have just served up thousands of dollars for charity, in the process nurturing the community with something money can't buy.

The recipes in this chapter are about bringing people together. Men love a hearty bean soup and the Mayor's Gumbo Coalition Seafood Gumbo. The rituals that we go through to create dishes like these speak to the rites, and Men are the head of the family and we are bringing back that feeling and showing the strength of the family unit. At Real Men Cook, we bring brothers together from all walks of life, and we become "a family of men."

# Carter Russell, Jr.
# The Brother's Homemade Pasta Sauce

Carter Russell, Jr.

**INGREDIENTS**

10 medium ripe tomatoes

¼ cup olive oil

2 tablespoons butter

3 onions, minced

1 stalk celery, chopped

2 green bell peppers, minced

4 garlic cloves, minced

2 tablespoons tomato paste

2 tablespoons Italian seasoning

¼ cup chopped fresh basil

1 bay leaf

½ cup dry red wine

Salt and black pepper

"I was raised from my teens by my dad. He had that tough love or that 'good evil' streak in him because he wanted me to make something of myself. I love music and all that it embodies, and I am living my dream working in the music industry. My dad never did understand what being in the music world meant to me, and he was opposed to my desire to pursue my own dream. In spite of his disapproval, he ran a tight ship at home and had dinner for us every evening despite the fact that he worked the four-to-midnight shift.

"My dad is now in his seventies and is an avid cook. He will give me a call at any given moment and say, 'Son, I've got some black beans and rice on the stove,' or 'I've got some navy beans,' or even 'I've got some spaghetti,' and I'm there. Like old times, but better.

"Family has always meant something very special to me. Our family is large, filled with great cooks and professional cooks. And I absorb as much information about cooking as I can from my aunts and uncles, 'cause when I cook, I have to get it right. Enjoying a good bottle of wine helps me get creative with my seasonings. My favorite gathering is Thanksgiving. Even though I don't have a favorite dish, I embrace the entire theme of cooking in abundance for giving thanks.

"One day, when I give up the music business, I just might convince my dad to move back to Jamaica and open up a little hut for breakfast and lunch featuring some local dishes like Jerk chicken and escovitch fish. After that, I'm gone; I'll spend the whole afternoon playing golf and sipping a Red Stripe beer."

1. Bring a pot of water to a boil. Have a large bowl of ice water ready. Plunge the whole tomatoes into the boiling water until the skin starts to pucker, about 1 minute. Remove with a slotted spoon and place in the ice water. When cool enough to handle, peel the tomatoes and squeeze out the seeds. Puree the tomatoes in a blender or food processor.

2. In a large skillet, heat the olive oil and butter and sauté the onions, celery, green pepper, and garlic over medium heat until the onion begins to caramelize, about 5 minutes. Add the pureed tomatoes. Stir in the

tomato paste, Italian seasoning, basil, bay leaf, and wine. Bring to a boil, then reduce the heat to low, cover, and let simmer for 2 hours. Season with salt and pepper to taste. Discard the bay leaf. Serve over your favorite pasta.

Makes 4 cups

**Carter Russell, Jr., was born in Chicago of Jamaican lineage. He is an icon in the music industry and an avid golfer. Russell participated in the first Real Men Cook event at the South Shore Cultural Center. He is married with one grown son.**

## Chaga Walton
# Chaga Walton's Stomping Salsa

Chaga Walton

"The dominant influence in my family on cooking was my mother. My mother's a fantastic cook and so was her mother; my maternal grandmother was known for her coconut cakes, and she and my mother did a lot of preserving as well. But those cakes and pastries . . . I mean we used to wait for the baked goods to come out of the oven, and before they even had a chance to cool, we'd be biting into a piece of them. My mother ended up having to cook a special tray: if she was doing stacked cakes, she'd make a special tray with one stack specifically for the children who were hovering around the oven just waiting for the delicious baked goods to be completed.

"I remember once when my mother was in the hospital delivering one of the many children that we've got in the family (there are eight of us in all), and my father was cooking. My father was never known to be a cook. He baked some biscuits, and those biscuits were as hard as a rock and I truly mean that. They were deep dark brown—and this was using white flour. You could drop them on the floor and hear the noise, just like a brick, and he really, *really* expected us to eat them. That was one of my worst food experiences!

3 cups diced tomato

1½ teaspoons adobo seasoning

1 cup diced green bell pepper

1 cup diced yellow bell pepper

⅓ cup chopped green onions (green and white parts)

1 garlic clove, finely chopped

1 jalapeño pepper, finely chopped

1 habanero pepper, finely chopped

2 tablespoons very finely chopped cilantro

One 6-ounce can tomato sauce (or you may substitute 1 small ripe tomato and 1 tablespoon extra-virgin olive oil)

1 teaspoon fresh lemon juice

"I enjoy Real Men Cook because of the camaraderie. There's a great group of men and women supporters that are always there to help to influence as well as to give you ideas and recipes, etc., and it's nice to know that somebody else is cooking besides you. So the money, the time, it's all well worth it, and we know that we're doing it for a charitable organization as well."

Place the tomatoes in a bowl; sprinkle with 1 teaspoon of the adobo seasoning. In a separate bowl, combine the bell peppers, green onions, garlic, jalapeño and habanero peppers, and the remaining ½ teaspoon adobo. Add the cilantro and tomato sauce. Add the tomatoes and lemon juice. Cover with plastic wrap and store overnight in the refrigerator, to allow the flavors to come together.

Makes about 5 cups. This salsa can be served with corn chips—lightly salted are recommended.

**Chaga Walton is my right *and* my left hand. There isn't anything he wouldn't do; he's just that sort of guy. He and his son, Kahari, are a pair; they truly go hand in hand. Like many of the brothers, Chaga will do whatever it takes to make the Real Men Cook event successful. He's my stand-in if need be. Chaga embodies the spirit of Real Men Cook and passes the word and the power on all year long.—K.K.M.**

# Special Barbecue Raccoon

### INGREDIENTS

1 raccoon (5 to 7 pounds), skinned and cleaned

2 cups white vinegar

2 cups beer

2 cups water

2 teaspoons cayenne pepper

1 teaspoon paprika

1 teaspoon white pepper

¼ cup liquid smoke

3 large sweet potatoes, quartered

Illinois congressman Danny K. Davis is very proud of his southern roots. He reminds us with this recipe that many of our family members once did and still continue to hunt and fish on the farm. Adding sweet potatoes gives this dish a sweet taste, which helps take away any gamy flavor.

1. Cut the raccoon into serving-size pieces (about 6). Combine the remaining ingredients (except the sweet potatoes), add the raccoon meat, and marinate for about 12 hours in the refrigerator.

2. Preheat the oven to 300°F.

3. Place the marinated meat (save the marinade) in a large flat baking pan and cover with a tent of aluminum foil. Roast for 2 hours. Turn and baste with marinade every 30 minutes. During the last 45 minutes of roasting add the sweet potatoes. Serve to all who dare to be bold!

Serves 4 to 6

## Donald Kindle
# Flying Pork Stir-fry

**INGREDIENTS**

2 tablespoons
vegetable oil

1 cup diced onion

¾ cup diced celery

1 cup diced carrots

1 cup diced green bell
pepper

1 pound chicken wings

1 pound hot links, cut
into 1-inch pieces

1 teaspoon cayenne
pepper

1 teaspoon garlic
powder

1 teaspoon salt

1 tablespoon dark
molasses

"I love to share stories about my father and his buddies and their experiences hunting and camping. For most of my adult life (thirty-five years), I have dedicated myself to working with young men, trying to give them the same rich experiences that I had with my dad and his friends. My dad was an Arkansas farmer, and his friends were from Alabama, Mississippi, and Tennessee. They were old-time southerners who just knew how to do stuff . . . and they just did it. Six or seven of us kids would get a chance to go along with these guys— these Real Men. They hunted, fished, made camp, then cooked some serious meals with the freshly caught game and fish, using herbs and spices, garlic, pepper, and bay leaves. To this day, I infuse those tastes and smells into my cooking.

"My favorite cooking utensil is the wok. I create magic with it, and I cook with the world's largest wok. I prepare exotic stir-fries over an open fire. Basically, I do things in a big way, and cooking this way lends itself to unique forms of expression. And this form of expression works well with the ladies, too! A big wok is a woman magnet. And this magnet works really well, as I have one of the longest lines at Real Men Cook!"

Heat the oil in a wok or large sauté pan. Add the onion, celery, carrots, and green pepper and sauté until slightly tender. Add the chicken wings and cook for 5 minutes. Add the hot links, cayenne, garlic powder, and salt. Continue stir-frying until all the ingredients are cooked. Stir in the molasses to coat the meat and vegetables. Serve over rice.

Serves 6

**Dr. Donald M. Kindle, a psychologist and the father of two sons, serves as a member of the board of directors of Real Men Charities, Inc., the nonprofit arm of Real Men Cook.**

Earl Carter and Ray Blackburn

# Chicken Breast Piccata and Golden Rice

### INGREDIENTS

12 boneless, skinless
chicken breasts (about
3¾ pounds)

½ teaspoon white
pepper

½ cup flour

¼ cup freshly grated
Parmesan cheese

6 large eggs, beaten

4 tablespoons (½ stick)
margarine

GOLDEN RICE:

4 tablespoons (½ stick)
margarine

⅓ cup diced onion

⅓ cup diced green bell
pepper

1 garlic clove, minced

⅓ cup canned
mushrooms, drained

⅓ cup diced red bell
pepper

3 to 4 cups long-grain
white rice

2 tablespoons chicken
base

Salt and black pepper

¾ teaspoon dried
oregano

½ teaspoon turmeric

1. Place the chicken breasts between dampened plastic. Flatten evenly with the flat part of a cleaver or knife. Season with the pepper and dredge in the flour; set aside in the refrigerator while you prepare the rice.

2. To make the rice: Heat the margarine in a skillet and sauté the onion, green pepper, garlic, and mushrooms. Bring 6 cups water to a boil in a saucepan and add the red pepper, rice, chicken base, salt and pepper to taste, the oregano, turmeric, and the sautéed onion mixture. Reduce the heat, cover, and let simmer for 15 to 20 minutes, until the liquid is absorbed and the rice is cooked.

3. Combine the cheese and eggs and mix thoroughly. Pour the mixture into a shallow pan. Soak the floured chicken breasts in the mixture for about 1 minute; the batter should completely cover the meat. Sauté the chicken in the margarine until golden brown on both sides. Serve with the rice.

Serves 12

"Fellas with Flava": DeRoy Bryant, Marc Campbell, Keith Cooper, Fred Dudley, Burt Jordan, and Percy Williams

# Real Men Homemade Sangria

## INGREDIENTS

1 bottle (1 liter) dry red wine

½ cup orange juice

½ cup cranapple juice

¼ cup sugar

¼ cup Triple Sec

¼ cup peeled and sliced apple

¼ cup diced peach

Orange slices, for garnish

This drink says it all. Enjoy it with friends!

Combine all of the ingredients except the orange slices in a large serving bowl and mix thoroughly. Serve chilled and garnish with orange slices.

Makes about 5 drinks

## Jimmy Toles

# Jimmy T's "On-Time" Bar-b-que Meats

**INGREDIENTS**

1 pound baby back ribs

1 pound pork ribs

1 pound beef ribs

1 whole chicken
(3 pounds), quartered

1 tablespoon garlic
powder

1 tablespoon onion
powder

1 tablespoon white
pepper

1 teaspoon meat
tenderizer

3 tablespoons paprika

1 teaspoon ground sage

1 tablespoon seasoned
salt

1 tablespoon salt

This recipe is great for a party. My suggestion is to double this recipe, because you know there are never enough ribs to go around.

1. Remove any excess fat from the ribs and chicken (a little can be left on for better cooking). Combine all of the seasonings and rub on the meat. Put the coated meat into resealable plastic bags and let marinate overnight in the refrigerator.

2. Heat the grill to medium. Place the ribs and chicken over the open fire. Let cook for about 1 hour, turning frequently. The meat and chicken should be completely cooked before adding any sauce. Once cooked, add your choice of barbecue sauce (on both sides), move to a cool part of the grill (or reduce the heat to low), and cook for 6 to 12 minutes.

Serves 10 to 12

# Tips for Making Great Food on the Grill

## by Rick Mays, Real Men Cook since 1992

My favorite way to prepare food is outside on my grill. I love the taste of grilled or broiled foods and the fact that cooking this way is healthier than pan-frying or deep-frying. However, just as with any other cooking method, it's possible to overcook your food, leaving it dry and unappetizing. Some people say food cooked over charcoal tastes better than food cooked on a gas grill. I think the only difference is that cooking with charcoal makes more work for the cook— lighting the fire, stirring the coals around, cleaning up the ashes. The fact is that many people, including me, use charcoal grills, and I've found the best grills to use are the kettle-style grills, like the Weber One-Touch. No, I don't work for Weber; I just think it's one of the best ones.

Some people are unsure of how to cook on a grill and therefore hesitate to try it, while others think they are masters but really don't have a clue. Well, I don't consider myself an expert by any stretch of the imagination, but I have found a few things that work well for me, and I would like to share them with you.

Let's start with cleaning your grill and lighting your fire.

Always start with a clean grill. The best thing to use when cleaning your grill is aluminum foil. *Do not use a metal brush.* Metal brushes are bad for your grill, because they scrape off the grill's protective finish, and this causes the grill to rust. Get a piece of foil about 18 inches long, crumple it up a little, and scrape off the cooked-on food. This will remove most of the food from the grill. Next, use a little dishwashing liquid and warm water and a sponge or dishcloth to remove the rest of the food and grease. Finish by using paper towels to wipe the grill dry.

If you need to clean the grill while you're cooking, just get some more foil and clean your grill right over the hot coals, *but be careful not to burn yourself.* Grab the foil with a pair of tongs and use the tongs to hold the foil, keeping your hands and arms from the heat. Finish by using a damp paper towel to wipe off excess grease. It's a good idea to clean the grill when starting to cook a different food. For instance, when you finish cooking chicken or ribs and want to switch to fish, you may want to do this.

To get that fire started using lighter fluid, pour the charcoal into the bottom of the grill and squeeze out some lighter fluid onto the coals. Try to get fluid on as many coals as possible, but don't use the whole can, okay? Next, stack the coals into a pyramid shape and let the lighter fluid soak into the coals for at least 5 minutes. It's important to let the fluid soak into the coals first, because if you light the coals right after you put lighter fluid on them, the lighter fluid will burn off before the coals have a chance to light. After a few minutes, put just a little bit more fluid on the coals and light them. Make sure the vent holes are open on the bottom so the airflow will help the fire to light quickly.

Do not put the cooking grill over the coals until the fire has burned out. The fire indicates that the lighter fluid is still burning, and if you put the grill over the fire, your grill will take on the flavor of lighter fluid, and lighter fluid is what your food will taste like. After the fire goes out, wait a few minutes, spread the coals out, and then place the cooking grill over the coals. You are ready to start cooking when most of the coals get a gray ash over them. You may need to stir the coals around to make the fire even before you start cooking.

You can control the temperature of the fire by opening or closing the vent holes in the top and bottom of the grill and by removing or replacing the top of the grill. For a hotter fire, make sure all the vent holes are wide open and the top is open or off. To cool the fire down, put the top back on and partially close the vent holes. If you close all the vent holes and put the top on, the fire will go out. If you get a flare-up while cooking, just sprinkle a little water in that area and/or place the top back on the grill.

If you need to add more coals, the best way is to carefully remove the cooking grill and pour in the new coals over the hot ones; within a few minutes they will light. **It is very dangerous to squirt lighter fluid on hot charcoal, so do not do it!**

If you want to use lighter fluid on the new coals you add, put the lighter fluid on the coals *before* you put them on top of the hot coals, then stand back and throw a lit match into the coals. Remember to let the fire go out before you continue cooking. To maintain airflow in the grill, remove ashes from the bottom of the grill often.

Now let's talk about utensils needed while cooking on the grill. First, invest in a good set (or two) of tongs. I use stainless steel, restaurant tongs. You can get them in some supermarkets or any restaurant supply store for about $5 to $12 a pair, depending upon the size and length. I use only tongs when handling food on or off the grill. *Do not use a fork!* When you stick a fork in the food, the holes made by the fork let the juices out, and this causes the food to become dry. The other items you'll need are a metal spatula, a sharp knife, a basting brush, and a water bottle to help put out any flare-ups.

## Want to add some smoke flavor to your food?

You can use hickory or mesquite wood chips or chunks. I like to use hickory for ribs and chicken, and mesquite for fish and other seafood. If you use wood chips, you can soak them in water for about 30 minutes before you put them on the hot coals. Soaking the chips first will cause them to produce smoke and prevent them from catching on fire when placed over the hot coals. The other way is to sprinkle the dry chips over the hot coals before you put the food on the grill, close the lid, and let the chips burn up. This will actually season the coals and still give you that smoked flavor. If you use wood chunks, do not soak them in water; just place a few of the chunks in after the coals are lit.

## How about some kabobs?

Shrimp, beef, chicken, vegetable, or a combination—here are a few tips. If you've ever tried cooking food on wooden skewers, you probably found out that the skewers caught on fire before the food was done. You can prevent this by soaking the skewers in water for about 20 to 30 minutes before you put the food on the skewers and onto the grill. To make sure all the food cooks evenly, make sure you use pieces that are about the same size and thickness so all the food on the skewer gets done at the same time. Beef, pork, and chicken take longer to cook than seafood, so cook seafood by itself. When placing shrimp on skewers, run the skewer through the shrimp in at least two places so the shrimp won't spin around when you try to turn the skewer over. Of course, you can mix in vegetables on your skewers for a nice-tasting, colorful dish. Before placing the skewers on the (cleaned) grill, oil the grill with some vegetable oil so they won't stick to the grill. You can do this by wetting a paper towel with a little vegetable oil and wiping it on the grill. *Use your tongs to hold the paper towel so you don't get burned.*

## Grilled fish—now, that's good eatin'!

The best type of fish to cook directly on the grill is fish that is meaty and firm (at least ¾ inch thick), like halibut, salmon, swordfish, shark, fresh tuna, or even catfish. Before you season or cook fillets, you should take a sharp knife and score (cut) the skin in two or three places about 2 inches apart. This technique will cause the fillets to stay flat and prevent them from curling up on the grill.

Using your basting brush, brush on a little melted butter or olive oil before you season your fish. After you season your catch, place it on an oiled grill, over medium-high heat, placing the fillets skin side up and on an angle so the edges don't fall between the grill. Close the cover, let the fish cook for about 2 minutes, and then take your spatula and just run it under the fish to loosen it from the grill, but don't move the fish. Hold on to it with the tongs while you slide the spatula under the fish. This gives you those nice grill marks. Do not turn it over yet; close the grill and let the fish cook for another 2 to 4 minutes. Brush on a little butter or olive oil and then turn the fish over. After you turn the fish over, let it cook for another 3 to 5 minutes and then remove it from the grill. When the fish starts to flake, it's done, so don't leave it on too long or it will start to fall apart and fall down into the fire.

## Adding Sauce

If you use barbecue sauce on your meats, put the sauce on *after* you take the food off the grill. Barbecue sauce has sugar in it that will caramelize, burn, and stick to the grill. A good way to finish ribs is to take them off the grill after they are cooked about three-quarters done (just as the bones begin to start showing on the edges). Cut the ribs apart into sections of one, two, or three ribs each. Put the ribs in a baking pan, add a little water to the pan, put your barbecue sauce on the ribs, cover the pan with foil, and place them in a preheated 325°F oven for about 20 minutes.

## Don't overcook your food.

When done properly, grilled food should always be moist, tender, and juicy. If you take the food off too early, and it's undercooked, that's okay; you can always put it back on the grill or finish it in the oven. But if food is overcooked, there's not too much you can do about that. A little trial and error will give you all the experience you need to know when something is done.

I hope these few tidbits help you to make better-tasting and better-looking food on the grill, and maybe even impress your friends and family at your next backyard barbecue. Don't be afraid to get out there and throw a few shrimp on the barbie, mate! *Happy grilling!*

# Joe W. Larché
# Atlanta Joe's N'awlins Spicy Jambalaya

INGREDIENTS

1 pound spicy hickory-smoked sausage, sliced on the diagonal into ¼-inch slices

1½ cups chopped onion

½ cup chopped green bell pepper

3 garlic cloves, minced

2 cups long-grain white rice

4 cups chicken broth

One 14½-ounce can stewed tomatoes, chopped, with juice

1 pound medium shrimp, with shells

2 tablespoons chopped green onions (green part)

Joe is the strong, silent type of guy. He's the administrative consultant to the commissioner of the Georgia Department of Labor and the City Colleges, and uses his position to affect children and the stability of families on the state and local levels. His wife, Diane, coordinates the Real Men Cook Event in Atlanta, making it not only the must-attend but also the "must-participate-in" event in town.

As his name might indicate, Joe is a product of N'awlins, where men cooked for family and friends in an environment that historically was restrictive, where families entertained at home, and where the confluence of cultures—African, Spanish, French, and Native American—made the Louisiana Purchase a bargain far beyond the pillagers' imagination. Joe is a product of the richness of this amalgamation; his cooking of jambalaya as well has his community involvement speaks volumes.—K.K.M.

1. Brown the sausage in a large Dutch oven or deep heavy skillet over medium-high heat. Drain, but reserve about 3 tablespoons of drippings. Add the onion and green pepper and sauté for 2 to 3 minutes, until tender. Add the garlic and sauté for 1 minute.

2. Add the rice and broth. Bring to a boil, reduce the heat to low, cover, and let simmer for 20 minutes. Stir in in the tomatoes, shrimp, and green onions and cook for 3 minutes, or just until the shrimp turn pink.

Serves 6 to 8

Lafayette Ford

# La La's Chicken Curry

"Much that I know about cooking came from my mom. She was a great cook, and she also possessed a great tolerance for the mess I used to make in the kitchen while attempting to prepare something edible.

"College life played a large part in helping me develop and hone my cooking skills. I was exposed to a variety of foods and cultures. My Japanese roommate, who was of mixed parentage, brought a broad knowledge of vegetables to our group of friends. My specialty was breakfast foods, and coupled with his knowledge of vegetables, we opened up a 'night kitchen' in our room. It didn't take long for word to get out, and students showed up throughout the night for one-bowl meals and late-night breakfasts.

"There is a strong link between what Real Men Cook does and what I do at home and in my profession as an educator with the Board of Education. My kids grew up in the midst of Real Men Cook and had a clear understanding of the tradition and how important it was for me to be involved, so they were happy to get me ready. I spend a lot of time with a variety of organizations with the best of intentions, but none of them generate the feelings that I get from this organization. Knowing that the men share the camaraderie, excitement, and anticipation of the people who attend, that everyone will enjoy the phenomenal food, and that nonprofits will benefit from this volunteer effort makes this entire effort very special.

"My wife and I lead very busy professional lives, and since I love to cook and do most of the cooking, I plan all of the meals and do most of the shopping. Since the age of twelve I have enjoyed this so much that I get up early or stay up late if need be to prepare for the next day. That's how dedicated I am. Even to the point of developing a barbecue sauce to sell to the public. It was my first entrepreneurial experience, selling this sauce by the gallon until I realized that the ingredients cost more than the selling price. The bottom line was that people enjoyed something that I'd created in the kitchen, and I have never stopped savoring that appreciation. The Real Men Cook Father's Day event enhances that admiration and appreciation."

1 whole chicken (3 to 4 pounds) cut up into serving pieces

¼ cup flour

Salt and black pepper

¼ pound (1 stick) unsalted butter

¼ cup chopped onion

¼ cup chopped celery

½ cup chopped green bell pepper

½ cup chopped red bell pepper

One 14½-ounce can stewed tomatoes

1 garlic clove, minced

2 to 3 teaspoons curry powder (mild or hot, to your taste)

½ teaspoon dried basil

½ teaspoon dried thyme

½ teaspoon dried oregano

1 cup chopped apple (peeled) (optional)

1. Preheat the oven to 350°F. Coat the chicken pieces with the flour and salt and pepper to taste. Heat 4 tablespoons of the butter in a heavy ovenproof skillet and brown the chicken. Remove the chicken from the pan and set aside.

2. Add the remaining 4 tablespoons butter to the skillet and sauté the onion, celery, and bell peppers over medium heat until they are tender. Add the tomatoes, garlic, curry powder, basil, thyme, and oregano. Return the chicken to the skillet, pour the tomato sauce over the chicken, and bake, uncovered, for 20 minutes, or until the chicken is tender. If you like, add the apple during the last ten minutes of cooking. Serve over rice.

Serves 6

## Kevin Ashford
# Row da Boat Curry Pineapple Shrimp

**INGREDIENTS**

1 pound large shrimp (16–20 count), peeled and deveined, with tails

1 teaspoon Creole seasoning

1 large pineapple

1 tablespoon extra-virgin olive oil

¾ cup chopped red bell pepper

¾ cup chopped green bell pepper

¾ cup chopped yellow bell pepper

¾ cup chopped onion

5 garlic cloves, minced

3 tablespoons Jamaican curry powder

¼ cup seafood or vegetable broth (water may be substituted)

1 teaspoon scotch bonnet pepper sauce

2 teaspoons chopped cilantro or parsley

If you can't take a quick trip to the islands, this dish will transport you to your favorite Caribbean destination. The combined flavors of fresh pineapple with scotch bonnet peppers and bell peppers will tantalize your taste buds. Put on some good reggae music and serve this with Sweet Basil's Rum Punch (see page 74)!

1. Season the shrimp with the Creole seasoning and set aside.

2. Quarter the pineapple (keep the leaves on the end of each piece for presentation). Remove the flesh and cut it into bite-size pieces. Set the shells and flesh aside.

3. Heat the olive oil in a large skillet over medium heat. Add the bell pepper, onion, and garlic and sauté until tender. Add the curry powder and broth and stir slowly; let simmer for 2 minutes. Add the shrimp, pineapple (with any juice), pepper sauce, and 1 teaspoon of the cilantro; continue to simmer until the shrimp are cooked.

4. Allow the mixture to thicken so it resembles a glaze. Spoon the shrimp and pineapple mixture onto the reserved pineapple shells and garnish with the remaining teaspoon cilantro. Serve with fried plantains and rice and peas.

Serves 4 to 6

Kevin Ashford and his wife, Kim Ashford

# Leonard Thomas
# Cool Hens in Jamaica

Leonard Thomas

**INGREDIENTS**

4 rock Cornish hens

Salt and freshly ground black pepper

3 to 4 tablespoons Walker's Wood jerk seasoning

⅓ cup dark rum

½ cup (1 stick) unsalted butter, melted

Paprika

**R**ock Cornish hens are a crossbreed of Cornish and Plymouth Rock chickens. They are small chickens that weigh between 1½ and 1¾ pounds and are between four and six weeks old. Because of their size, one bird is usually just enough for one person. Their young age makes them very tender. They are quick and easy to prepare.

1. Wash the hens, pat dry, and cut off the wing tips. Place your fingers between the skin and meat to loosen the skin around the hens; season with salt and pepper. In a bowl, mix the jerk seasoning and rum; rub some under and over the skin—massage in well. Place the hens in a large plastic bag and let marinate overnight in the refrigerator. (When I make this recipe, I marinate the hens for 2 days so that the seasoning really penetrates the meat.—L.T.)

2. Preheat the oven to 375°F.

3. Place the hens on a rack in a roasting pan and pour about ½ cup water in the bottom of the pan to keep the smoke down. Pour the melted butter over the hens and sprinkle on a little paprika. Roast the hens for about 35 to 40 minutes, until the juices run clear.

Serves 4

**Leonard Thomas—Harlem's famous "Chicken Man"—is a committed member of our New York cadre of cooks. He has served as event spokesperson and has participated for five consecutive years.**

## Moses White

# Florida Boy Baked Beans

**INGREDIENTS**

2 cups granulated sugar

½ cup packed dark brown sugar

2 cups molasses

2 tablespoons mustard

8 cups ketchup

1 pound ground beef

Two 28-ounce cans baked beans

4 slices bacon

These beans are great for a picnic, or even a lazy winter day. They are easy to make and the kids will love them.

1. Preheat the oven to 250°F.

2. Mix all of the ingredients well in a 12 by 8-inch baking dish. Place the bacon on top and bake for 1 to 1½ hours.

Serves 8 to 10

## Senator Emil Jones

# Chicago Shrimp Creole

**INGREDIENTS**

¼ pound (1 stick) butter

2 cups chopped onion

1 cup chopped green bell pepper

1 cup chopped celery

Lawry's seasoned salt

Cayenne pepper

2 bay leaves

2 pounds tomatoes, peeled, seeded, and chopped

1 tablespoon chopped garlic

The Honorable Emil Jones is the president of the Illinois senate. Jones, a longtime politician, is very active and dedicated to his constituents. He is a driving force in furthering the positive images of African American men. His devotion to his family and his dedication to the state and his community leave an indelible mark on the strengths and commitments of what Real Men believe in.

Creole cooking represents a mélange of the African, French, and Spanish cultures that settled in New Orleans in the 1800s. This style of cooking showcases the diverse flavors that have made it one of the most popular styles of cooking today. This recipe has a heaping full of Chicago flavor to it.

1. Melt the butter in a large saucepan over medium heat. Add the onion, green pepper, and celery; season with salt and cayenne to taste. Sauté

Dash of Worcestershire sauce

Dash of hot sauce

2 tablespoons flour

2½ pounds large shrimp, peeled and deveined

2 tablespoons Creole Seasoning/Bayou Blast (below)

2 tablespoons finely chopped green onions (green and white parts)

1 tablespoon chopped fresh parsley, plus extra for garnish

until the vegetables are soft, 6 to 8 minutes. Stir in the bay leaves, tomatoes, and garlic. Taste, and season again with salt and cayenne, if needed. Bring the mixture to a boil, reduce the heat, and let simmer for 15 minutes. If it becomes too dry, add some water. Season the mixture with Worcestershire sauce and hot sauce.

2. Whisk the flour with 1 cup water in a small bowl, then add to the tomato mixture and continue to cook for 5 to 6 minutes.

3. In a separate bowl, season the shrimp with the Creole Seasoning/ Bayou Blast. Then add the shrimp to the mixture and continue to cook for 4 to 6 minutes, until the shrimp turn pink and curl up. Stir in the green onions and parsley. Garnish with chopped parsley.

Serves 4

INGREDIENTS

2½ tablespoons paprika

2 tablespoons salt

2 tablespoons garlic powder

1 tablespoon black pepper

1 tablespoon onion powder

1 teaspoon cayenne pepper

1 tablespoon dried oregano

1 tablespoon dried thyme

## Creole Seasoning/Bayou Blast

Combine all of the ingredients and mix well. Store in an airtight container.

Makes ⅓ cup

## Marc H. Morial

# Mayor's Gumbo Coalition Seafood Gumbo

**INGREDIENTS**

½ cup vegetable oil

½ cup flour

1 cup chopped onion

½ cup chopped green bell pepper

1 teaspoon dried thyme

1 tablespoon chopped basil

2 bay leaves

4 quarts seafood stock, made from heads and shells of peeled shrimp

1 pound turkey sausage, cut into 2-inch pieces

4 jumbo crabs (1 to 1½ pounds each)

2 pounds medium shrimp (with heads), peeled and deveined

3 catfish fillets (1½ pounds), cut into cubes

1 pound okra, cut into 1-inch pieces

1 tablespoon chopped garlic

Salt and black pepper

1 pound oysters, shucked and cleaned

"Our coalition is like gumbo. It's got a little of this and a little of that. You know how gumbo is—it takes a variety of ingredients to make a good gumbo."

1. Heat the oil in a skillet and add the flour to make a roux. Stir constantly until very brown, about 15 to 20 minutes.

2. Reduce the heat and add the onion, green pepper, thyme, basil, and bay leaves. Slowly add the stock, stirring constantly. Bring to a boil, then add the sausage, crabs, shrimp, and catfish. Reduce the heat and simmer for 10 minutes, then add the okra, garlic, and salt and pepper to taste; cook for 10 minutes. Add the oysters and cook for about 2 minutes. If the gumbo is too thick, add more stock. If you desire, additional seasonings, such as Old Bay Seasoning or gumbo filé, may be added to satisfy your personal taste. Serve over steamed rice.

Serves 8 to 10

**Marc H. Morial, former mayor of New Orleans, is currently the president and chief executive officer of the National Urban League. He hosted Real Men Cook for three consecutive years and remains a friend and supporter of the spirit and intent of the organization.**

Paul Madyum

# Original Muslim Bean Soup

**INGREDIENTS**

1½ pounds small navy beans

½ cup chopped celery

1½ cups chopped onion

1¼ cups chopped green bell pepper

½ cup sliced carrots

1 medium garlic clove, chopped

1½ cups chopped tomato

Sea salt

Turmeric

Cayenne pepper

½ cup (1 stick) butter or ½ cup olive oil (optional)

This recipe is easy to prepare, is very inexpensive, and has been a staple in the American Muslim community for more than sixty years. Navy beans (small pea size) are rich in protein, carbohydrates, and minerals, so this soup provides an overall balanced food for the diet. The vegetables in this recipe add nutritional value. This soup is so hearty that it can be used as a main course with the addition of brown rice and a large salad. Make a second pot and give to a friend. This is a great dish for those cold and blustery winter days.

1. Wash the beans a couple of times to remove the dirt and debris, then soak them for 4 hours. Drain the beans, place them in a large pot, and cover with enough water so that the water line is an inch or so over the beans. Bring to a boil over low heat. Skim foam from the top and continue to cook for 30 minutes, until they are slightly cooked but not done.

2. Add the celery, onion, pepper, carrots, garlic, and tomato, and salt, turmeric, and cayenne to taste; continue to cook until the beans are done, about 30 minutes, or until they begin to break. Make sure there is adequate liquid. It is important not to let the soup thicken; add more water, if needed. Add the butter, if using, and fold into the soup. Turn off the heat. Let cool for about 10 minutes, then pour soup through a food mill *(for modern cooks, you may use a blender or a food processor . . . ugh!!)* at low speed. The soup will thicken naturally. Stir well and enjoy!

Serves 4 to 6

**The late Honorable Elijah Muhammad said that if we would raise our children on this soup, we could raise a mighty nation; they would be healthy enough to live 120 years.**

Shelly Wynter

# Shelly's Stuffed Snapper

## INGREDIENTS

1 whole red snapper
(2 to 3 pounds)

1 teaspoon black
pepper

1 teaspoon ground
allspice

1⅓ cups barbecue sauce

1⅓ cups teriyaki sauce

3 cups seasoned bread
crumbs

1 teaspoon onion
powder

1 tablespoon dried
oregano, crumbled

3 tablespoons butter

¼ pound crabmeat

¼ pound large shrimp,
peeled and deveined

¼ pound catfish,
cut into fillets

A whole red snapper makes a beautiful presentation. It is available year-round and is suitable for virtually any cooking method.

1. Season the inside of the snapper with the black pepper and allspice. Combine ⅓ cup of the barbecue sauce and ⅓ cup of the teriyaki sauce and spread the mixture on the inside and outside of the fish. Cover the fish with plastic wrap and place in the refrigerator for 1 hour.

2. Combine the bread crumbs, onion powder, oregano, and the remaining cups of barbecue sauce and teriyaki sauce.

3. Preheat the oven to 300°F.

4. Heat the butter in a skillet and sauté the crabmeat, shrimp, and catfish for 5 minutes, then add to the stuffing mixture. Take the snapper out of the refrigerator and put the stuffing inside and close with toothpicks. Pour any excess stuffing over the fish. Wrap in aluminum foil and make sure that it is tightly sealed. Bake for 25 minutes (or cook on the grill for 30 to 40 minutes).

Serves 6

Vincent Alexandria

# Mexican Corn Bread

INGREDIENTS

2 pounds ground beef

Seasoned salt

1¼ cups diced onion

1 tablespoon sliced
garlic

1¼ cups diced green
bell pepper

Three 15½-ounce cans
Del Monte Fiesta Corn

5 boxes Jiffy corn bread
mix

½ pound Kraft Velveeta
cheese, cut into chunks

## When Brothers Meet

By Vincent Alexandria

*When brothers meet, it is an exchange of souls,*
*The depth of intellectuality unfolds,*
*Speaking, seeking, tweaking plans,*
*Helping each other to understand,*
*Eye to eye and attentively listening,*
*Feeding on knowledge, wisdom, and beckoning,*
*The ancestors from our native land to clear our minds,*
*So dialog is processed and objectives agreed upon with shaken*
*    hands in present time,*
*Respect for what each bring to the table,*
*Equipping each other and making us stable,*
*In careers we wish to pursue,*
*Pushing each other up in all things that we do.*

1. Preheat the oven to 375°F. Butter a 12 by 8-inch baking pan.

2. Season the ground beef with seasoned salt to taste and place in a large skillet. Add the onion, garlic, and green pepper; cook over medium-high heat until the meat is brown.

3. Drain the corn, reserving the juice from *one* of the cans; set aside. Empty the corn bread mix into a large bowl and mix according to package directions. Add the reserved corn juice to the batter and stir.

3. Put half the corn bread batter into the prepared pan. Evenly distribute the beef on top of the batter. Place the corn over the beef. Scatter the cheese on top of the corn. Top with the remaining batter. Bake for about 50 minutes, or until the top is golden brown. Let cool for about 10 minutes and serve.

Serves 8 to 10

# Afterword

## Useni Eugene Perkins

D espite denied opportunities to develop their true potential, black men in America have made contributions to the world that contradict the myth that they are lazy, incompetent, and lacking a work ethic. Their contributions range from performing the world's first open-heart surgery (Dr. Daniel Hale Williams, 1893) to inventing the gas mask (Garrett A. Morgan) to designing the first refrigerator (John Standard).

However, these feats should not be seen as a fertile revelation. As descendants of the world's first classic civilization, ancient Kemet (Egypt, 3100 B.C.), black men have always demonstrated an extraordinary propensity to be creative and resourceful. The building of the first Pyramids, the invention of mathematics and a calendar, and the development of chemistry and hieroglyphics are a few of the achievements made by black men predating the civilizations of ancient Greece and Rome.

Although black men were brought to America as slaves to labor in the cotton fields, many retained the specialized skills that they had mastered in their native African homeland. Because they possessed these specialized skills, many African men worked as masons, carpenters, blacksmiths, and artisans. In particular, their skill in masonry helped to build many of the impressive mansions common to the South during the antebellum period. The skills of black men also played a major role in the building of America's vast railroad empire that led to her being a leader in the industrialized world. Lerone Bennett, Jr., historian and senior editor of *Ebony* magazine, said, "The United States, Brazil and other parts of South America are all indebted to [black] labor." Indeed, the sweat of black men was a formidable factor in the making of America.

Consider another popular myth: black men have been emasculated because of their attachment to a matriarchal family structure. Empirical evidence tends to refute this. To be more accurate, the traditional structure of the black family was a utilitarian one that fostered cooperative relationships in decision making and the performing of domestic tasks by both genders. Due to the adverse effect of slavery, the black family had to develop its own unique structure to cope with oppression. Under this structure, black men performed a variety of domestic chores, prominent among them being the preparation of meals when it was necessary. This is one reason many black men have developed excellent culinary skills. I can recall that despite the fact that my mother was a superb cook, my appetite increased enormously when I knew my father was going to prepare a meal.

Many of the world's most prestigious restaurants and hotels have benefited from the culinary skills of black men, indeed of men in general. Black men have taken great pride in their cooking and are unabashed about letting others know it. In fact, they would often engage in braggadocio with other men to show off their culinary skills. To be able to "burn" in the black community was a skill that gained one both recognition and prestige.

No doubt many of the men participating in Real Men Cook have engaged in this ritual. In so doing, their manhood is still intact because they realize that cooking is not an affront to their masculinity. Rather, it is an avocation or a vocation in which men partake because of their domestic responsibilities or for the personal satisfaction they receive in preparing food for their families and others.

It is in this spirit and tradition that we celebrate the Real Men who cook, and look up to them as models for generations to come.

# Roll Call

A. Bruce Crawley
A. Robert Brown
A. G. Magee, Jr.
A. T. Coleman
Aaron Cain
Aaron Caldwell
Aaron Junior
Abe Mack
Actor Arif S. Kinchen
Adam Bush
Adolpho Love
Ahmad Ade
Akil Kamal
Akil Kamu
Al Bell
Al Kelley
Al Kelly
Al Palmer
Al Potter
Al Ross
Alan Hunt
Alan Johnson
Albert Brown
Albert Brown, M.D.
Albert McBeth
Albert N. Logan
Albert Reese, Sr.
Albert Thomas
Albert Williams
Alejandro Correa
Alex Curtis
Alfred (Emanuel)
   Morris
Alfred Crenshaw
Alfred Gordon
Alfred Harris
Alfred Jackson
Alfred May
Alfred Neloms, D.N.
Alfred Wilson
Allen Hill
Allen Johnston
Allen Kemp
Allen L. Broods, Jr.
Allen Lane
Allen Tanner
Allison Debonnet, Jr.

Alonzo Brown
Alonzo Jones III
Alpha Phi Alpha
   Fraternity, Inc.
Althea Stokes
Alton Smith
Alvin Bell, Jr.
Alvin Higgins
Alvin Rogers
Alvin Watson
Amahde Duncan
Amanarh Kisseih
Ameer Salaam
Amir Sealy
Amos Reed
Andre Griffen
Andre Joyner
Andre Shepard
Andrew Duhé
Andrew Gordon
Andrew Henderson
Andrew Lindsey
Andrew London
Andrew Walker
Anthony Atkins
Anthony Aubry
Anthony Bond
Anthony Brooks
Anthony Burrell
Anthony Gabriel
Anthony Glover
Anthony Grady
Anthony Heflin
Anthony Jackson
Anthony Jernagin
Anthony Johnson
Anthony Joiner
Anthony Kelley
Anthony Ladson
Anthony Lewis
Anthony Lipscomb
Anthony McClary
Anthony Navarro
Anthony Overton
Anthony Patterson
Anthony Range
Anthony Roberson

Anthony Ross
Anthony Streets
Anthony Wiley
Antoine P. Hopkins
Antone Miles
Antonio Matthews
Antonio Tate
Archie N. Grant
Archie Sanders
Archie Tolar
Arnell Chaney
Arnell Everett
Arnold Binkley
Art Clay
Art Sims
Arthur C. Teele
Arthur Clay
Arthur Davis
Arthur Fennell
Arthur L. Coates
Arthur Thomas
Artis Owens
Artis Simpson
Arturo D. Hill IV
Atlanta Hawks
Atty. Anthony Carr
Augustus Tolson, Jr.
Austin Cunningham
Avell Collier
Aubrey Washington
Ayo Ogunduyile
Azziem Ali
B'yon P. Hairstoni
Baché Holland
Barbara Guillory
Baron James
Barry Wooden
Basil Avery
Basil Brathwaite
Bempa
Ben M'tundu
Benjamin Mchie
Benny Franklin
Bernard Geiger
Bernard Guinyard
Bernard Johnson
Bernard Jordan

Bernard Key
Bernard Levy
Bernard Rivers
Bert Matuszoki
Big Oomp Records
Bill Borden
Bill Brown
Bill Campbell
Bill Davis
Bill Edwards
Bill English
Bill Hubbard
Bill Keyes
Bill Merritt
Bill Palmer
Bill Reynolds
Bill Sweeney
Bill Williams
Bill Zollars
Billy Barnes
Billy Hubbard
Billy Montgomery
Billy Morrow
Blair Talmadge
Bob Klutch
Bob McCaskill
Bob Nash
Bob Scott
Bob Starks
Bobby Booker
Bonny Rice
Brad Boots Taylor
Brad Goldsby
Brad Tucker
Brandon Joe
Brian Barry
Brian Butcher
Brian Coleman
Brian Durrell
Brian Harvey
Brian Hill
Brian McCinic
Brian McClenic
Brian Moody
Brian Peterkin
Brian Swift
Brian Washington

## Al Bell

A businessman, financier, and community philanthropist, Al Bell is cut from seasoned wood. Having raised and educated his children, and opened and closed several businesses, he is in that nothing-to-prove zone. Al gives freely of his time and resources to deserving organizations including the Rotary, YMCA, and Real Men Charities Inc. Like most other brothers, Al is a silent champion who enjoys seeing something good and positive come out of the energy he shares. He doesn't need the fanfare, just the personal gratification that a good deed has been done and is successful.

—K.K.M.

Brinston Williams
Broderick Rufflin
Bruce Caldwell
Bruce Daugherty
Bruce Duane Hall
Bruce Hall
Bruce L. Chaney
Bruce N. Talbert
Bruce Rush
Bruce Thomas
Bruce Tolbert
Bruce Wheatley
Bryant Echols
Burnett Newkirt
Burt Jordan
Byrie Colley
Byron Brady
Byron Foster
Byron White
C. Von
C. T. Martin
Cake Men Raven
Caleb Rutledge
Caluita Federick-
  Sowell
Cam Castle
Carl A. Jenkins
Carl A. Lee

Carl Bell
Carl Johnson
Carl Lee Johnson,
  Jr.
Carl Thomas
Carl Watts
Carl West
Carl Wolf
Carlos Jones
Carlos Turner
Carlton Backs
Carlton Dudley
Carlton Dudley, Jr.
Carlton Hargo
Carlton Moore
Carol Adams
Carolyn Shelton
Carter Russell
Cary A. Holman, Jr.
Cary Earle
Ceasar Mitchell
Cecelia Houston
  Torrence
Cedric Knott
Cedric Lyons
Ces Lopez
Chaga Walton
Channon Draper

Charles Albert
Charles Cash
Charles Davis
Charles Eugene
Charles Grant
Charles Harrison
Charles Headen
Charles Hinton
Charles Horbowski
Charles Milliner
Charles Parker
Charles Phillips
Charles Rambo
Charles Ronald
  Sherrell
Charles Sherrel II
Charles Smith
Charles White
Charlie Richardson
Chef Sherman
  Sharpe
Chef Washington
Chester Logan
Chistopher K.
  Jenkins
Chris Booth
Chris Brewer
Chris Cognac
Chris Gabriel
Chris Hawkins
Chris Lewis
Chris McEvilley
Chris Moore
Chris Robinson
Chris Wafer
Chris Whalum
Chris Williams
Christian Franco
Christopher Forbes
Christopher Jones
Christopher Katz
Christopher Kay
Christopher
  McFarland
Christopher
  Ridenhour
Chuck Pallid
Chuck Smith
Chukudi Chinwah
Chuma Smith
Clarence Eddie
Clarence Lewis
Clarence Lott III
Clarence Moss

Clarence Winbush,
  Jr.
Clark James
  Simmons III
Clark Simmons
Claude Gibson
Cliff Levington
Clifford Rome
Clifton Samuels
Clifton Underwood
Clifton Washington
Clifton West
Clint Evans
Clinton Evans
Clinton Moore
Clyde Thompson
Colby Colb
Coleman
  McCormick
Colone Pearson
Columbus T.
  Jenkins, Jr.
Conrad R. Harris
Corey Allen
Corey Kirkendoll
Corey Smith
Corey Tyiska
Cornelius Simon
Cory Ash
Craig Gilmore
Craig Hodges
Craig May
Curlee Adams
Curtis Chancellor
Curtis Jones
Curtis Pearson
Curtis Simpson
Curtis Singleton
Cuttie Bacon
Cyrus Pots
D. C. Crenshaw
Daffrey Jackson
Dalandis Neeley
Dale Long
Dale Sims
Damon Bailey
Dan Graham
Dan Perkins
Dan Washington
Dana E. Luellen
Dana Herbert
Daniel Cherry III
Daniel Craddock
Daniel Dixon, M.D.

Danniel Haymon
Danny D. Slider, Sr.
Danny Davis—
	Congressman
Danny Graham
Danny Mason
Dannye. Ingram
Dargan Burns
Darian Harrington
Darick Simpson
Darien Wilson
Darnell Green
Darnell Kaigler
Darrel Smith
Darrell Bragg
Darrell Newell
Darrell Thompson
Darren Nolen
Darrick Hargro
Darron O. Lewis
Darryl Dennard
Darryl Ewell
Darryl Hobson
Darryl J. Holloway
Darryl Johnson
Darryl Jones
Darryl Merchant
Darryl Mims
Darryl Powell
Darryl Roberts
Darryl Sams
Darryl V. Hunter
Darryl Williams
Dave Brown
Dave Davis
Dave Gupta
Davian Freeman
David Anderson
David Allum
David Battle
David Bereal
David Berry
David Blackmon
David Crenshaw
David Dalrymple
David Day
David Decuir
David Ferguson
David Freeman
David Handy
David Haynes
David L. Smith
David Lee Baron
David Lilly

David Manuel
David Marin
David Mims
David Mitchell
David Norman
David Robinson
David White
D. C. Wiliams
Deadrian Troupe
Dean Wade
Dee McKinzie
Delandis Neeley
Del-Re Dudley
Delroy Christian
Delvon Jackson
Denise Carter
Denise Mitchem
Dennis Gardin
Dennis Hinton
Dennis Jackson, Sr.
Dennis Matthews
Denver Jackson
Dereck Caldwell
Derek Davis
Derek Dean
Derek Hicks
Derek James
Derek Lowery
Derek Taylor
Deroy Bryant
Derrick Angus
Derrick Boazman—
	Councilman
Derrick Brockman
Derrick Brown
Derrick M. Hicks
Derrick Merritt
Derrick Michael
	Hicks
Derrick Robinson
Derrick Salahhuddin
Derrick Williams
Derrick Winkfield
Derrie Hale, Jr.
Derryl Reed
Detroit Omega
Devin McCormick
Dewayne Conigan
Dexter Porter
Dhati Price
Diarr Castello
Dicky Kelly
Dimitrious Oliver
Dion Glover

## Brian Bridges

"I started out cooking with my mother. She had five children, and I'm the second oldest. I cooked with my grandmother as well. My grandmother was blind and has never seen any of her children or grandchildren.

"My grandmother would always say, 'Give me a pinch of this and a pinch of that.' As I got older, I started to cook with Hunter—that's my grandfather. The Wild Game Man (which he was also known as) would go out for three days at a time and catch the food way out somewhere—pig, turtle, raccoon, rabbit, goose, chicken, duck, etc. If we could eat it, he would catch it and cook it. So that is why I'm here. I love to cook. Whether it's for family, friends, reunions, or for a large group, I'm there to share my family cooking."

Doc Brown
Dominique Wilkins
Don Bickham
Don Burnett, Jr.
Don Cleveland
Don Houston
Don Jackson
Don Johnson
Don Kendall
Don Kindle
Don Lewis
Don Pearce
Don Quaite
Don Rashid
Don Rivers
Don Rose
Don Walton
Don Wilson
Donald Godbold,
	M.D.
Donald Howard
Donald J. Dew
Donald Jarmond

Donald Johnson
Donald Jones
Donald Snipes
Donald Walker, Jr.
Donald Wilbon
Donald Yarbrough
Donnell Spencer
Donnie Hinton, Sr.
Donnie Mitchell
Dorian Jones
Douglas Alan-Mann
Doyle Johnson
Duane West
Dushun Mosley
Dwaine Miller
Dwayne Caraway
Dwayne L. Bentley
Dwayne Morris
Dwayne Shen
Dwight Eaton
Dwight Jones
E. Jerome Williams
E. Steven Collins

E. J. Junior Smith
Earl Bell
Earl Bowers
Earl Caldwell
Earl Calloway
Earl Carter
Earl McGhee
Earmer Young
Earnest Daniel, Jr.
Ebenezer AME
    Church
Ed Beavers
Ed Jeffrie
Ed Keene
Edcardo Odom
Eddie Brown, Jr.
Eddie Dean
Eddie Hayes
Eddie L. Cleaves, Jr.
Eddie L. Kornegay, Jr.
Eddie L. Maddox
Eddie L. Wright
Eddie Levert
Eddie Parker
Eddie Walker
Edmund Howard
Edward Broom, Jr.
Edward Lance
Edward P. McCombs,
    Jr.
Edward Willis
Edwin Wardlaw
Ejah Jacobs, Jr.
Eldred B. Taylor
Eldred B. Taylor,
    M.D.
Elihu Blanks
Elliot Francis
Elliott Johnson
Elmer Smith
Elonzo Watson
Elven Walker III
Elven Walker, Jr.
Elvis Williams
Elwood Washington
Emil Godfrey, Jr.
Emmanuel Gillespie
Erhaboor Onawu
Eric A. McMiller
Eric Adkison
Eric Burke
Eric Daniels
Eric Jones
Eric Lane

Eric McKissack
Eric Osley
Eric Paris
Eric Span
Eric Wilson
Eric Y. Brown
Eric E. Daniels
Erich Harvey
Erick Burton
Erwin L. Smith, Sr.
Eugene Lockhart
Eugene Morris
Eugene Raymon
Eugene Sawyer
Eunice Chaney
Eura Wilford
Everett McLeary
Everett Rand
Ewan L. Edwards
Excel Sharrieff
Ezra Powell
F. Spider McCoy
Fabrizo Passalacqua
Faithy Harris
Faron Hill
Farrid Nabahar
Felix Burrows, Jr.
Felix Ford
Felton Armand
Femi Olughesan
Fernando Jones
Fernando
    O'Loughlin
Fletcher Smith
Flowers Jenkins
Floyd Carter
Floyd Hudson
Floyd Wallace
Floyd Webb
Floyd Wright
Fonge Dixion
Forest Johnson
Foundation, Inc.
    (DOFI)
Francisco Gonzalez
Frank Champlin
Frank Chaplin
Frank Cortez
Frank Frazier
Frank Hayden, Jr.
Frank McKinley
Frank Medina
Frank Mitchell
Frank Pete, Jr.

Frank Ski
Frank Whitehead
Frankie McMillian
Franklin Love
Franklin Taylor
Franklin Victory
Fred Dodson
Fred Dodson III
Fred Dodson IV
Fred Dudley
Fred Howard
Fred Jean Marie
Fred Moore
Fred Nance
Fred Wilson
Fred Worrell
Freddie McCoy
Frederick C. Jackson
Frederick Dais
Frederick Gamble
Frederick Major
Fredrick Dias
Fritz Neukam
Gabriel Hamer
Gabriel Kendall
Gairy Fuller
Galatian Norman
Garland Morgan
Gary Clayton
Gary Matthews
Gary Minger
Gary S. Heflin
Gary Sheffield
Gary Wilkerson
Gavriel Moyo
Gaylord Minett
Gene Sawyer-
    Mayor
Geof Fletcher
Geoffrey Bassett
George Bowman
George Brown
George C. Mitchell
George C. Neal
George C. Whitfield,
    Jr.
George Daniels
George Duncan
George Gossett, Jr.
George Hudson
George Payton
George W. Daniels
George Williams
Gerald Cooper

Gerald Jackson
Gerald Levert
Gerald McCullar
Gerard Polite
Gil Robertson
Glen Brooks
Glenn DaCruz
Glover Anthony
Godfrey Mason
Gordon Keith
Gordon Marshall
Graig Morrer
Graig Reese
Grant Branch III
Greg Allen
Greg Chatman
Greg DeShields
Greg Garrett
Greg Jones
Greg King
Greg Pridgeon
Gregg Peters
Gregory B. Caldwell
Gregory Hardin, Sr.
Gregory Hinton
Gregory K. Hardin
Gregory Lester
Gregory Manley
Gregory Penn
Gregory S. Braswell,
    Jr.
Gregory Simpson
Gregory White
Gregory Williams
Guy Dunn
Guy Toley
Guy W. Hodge
H. Lamar Willis
Hadid Alshura
Hakim Surmon
Hanif Shrif-Ali
Hank Johnson
Hank Steward
Hank Stewart
Hannibol Sullivan
Hansel A. Stinson
Hari Brown
Harlan Gathright
Harold Hambrick
Harold Johnson
Harold Metts
Harold Morris
Haroon Ali
Harrell Varner

Harrison James
  Phillips
Harrison Sherman
Harry Mays
Harry McCord
Harry Phillips
Harry Ramos
Hayward Suggs
H. D. McKenzie
Henry Brown
Henry Coaxum
Henry Meyer
Henry Mire
Henry Richards
Herb Kent
Herbert E. Williams,
  Jr.
Herbert Alexander,
  Sr.
Herbert Allen
Herbert Gears
Herbert Sanders
Herbert Wilkerson
Herman Brewer
Heurnton Brown
Hisham Tawfiq
Hollis Wilson
Honorable Alex Z.
  Talmadge
Honorable James
  DeLeon
Honorable W. Curtis
  Thomas
Horace Broy, D.D.S.
Hotep
Howard A. Tanner
Howard F. Chisholm
Howard Hill
Howard Paige
Howard Simmons
Howard T. Logan
Hubert Eddings
Ibn Sharrieff
Imara Canady
Iota Phi Theta
Ira Linton
Ira Strong
Ira Wilson
Isaiah Franklin
Israel Rodriquez
Issac Johnson
Issac McKinney
Ivory Young
J. Fidal Young

J. Martin Lett
J. Steven Strawbridge
  IV
J. Vincent Marcus III
J. Walter Hale
J. Martin Lett
Jack Johnson
Jack Peters
Jack W. Wheeler
Jackson Floyd
Jamal Broy
Jamal Oliver
Jamal Starr
Jamar Bates
James "J" Love
James Archier
James Bacchues
James Battieste
James Brevard
James Cannon
James Chandler
James Chandler,
  M.D.
James Couch
James Dorsett
James Dunlap
James Dyson
James E. Allen, Jr.
James English
James Felton
James Fletcher
James Gary
James Heath
James JB Brown
James Jones
James K. Davis
James LaStrap
James Mann
James Mattz
James McHenry
James Moore
James Moye
James Odoms
James P. Chandler
James P. Harris
James R. Brown
James Stewart
James Thurman
James Walker
James Washington
James Williams
James Willis
James Yerger
Jamie

# Emmett T. Vaughn

**Real Men Cook**

"Where has all the time gone? A full sixteen years have passed since the original Real Men of Real Men Cook took to the floor of Chicago's legendary Museum of Science and Industry. There were Chicago professional athletes, congressmen, media celebrities, and *me*! (And my undisputed best-ever chili.)

"I hardly knew Kofi and Yvette then, being a relatively new Chicagoan. Little did I know that this event that I was asked to participate in would yield so many rich and long-term friendships. Having the opportunity these many years later to remain active in Real Men Cook and seeing 'them little kids' (including my own) actually participating now as young adults truly feeds (no pun intended) my spirit.

"Looking back at this time in our lives, it is possible that the legacy that is Real Men Cook could end up as an understated happening. But the message and opportunity the experience affords 'us mens' now is to actively contribute love, warmth, and energy into that which feeds our spirit, family, and community. Preparing food or a meal merely is a vehicle by which we can express the strength of our real inner man."

Jamika Pessoa
Jarryl Anderson
Jason Allen
Jason Carter
Jason Flowers
Jason Motley
Jason Terry
Jay Carter
Jay Rich of Roscoe's
    Chicken & Waffles
Jay Williams
Jaye Archer
Jean Alphonse
Jean B. Ware
Jeff Fleming
Jeff Harris
Jeff Harrison
Jeff Lewis
Jeff McCann
Jeff Scales
Jeff Weir
Jefferson Haskins
Jeffery Gray
Jeffery Henderson
Jeffery Scales
Jeffrey Davis
Jeffrey Dugas, M.D.
Jeffrey Flagg
Jeffrey Trochach
Jeffri Epps
Jeno Jones
Jerald Morgan
Jeremy E. Hildreth
Jermaine Dunn
Jermaine Jones
Jerome Barksdale
Jerome Harrison
Jerome Payne
Jerome Sims
Jerome Thomas
Jerome Wade
Jerome Watts
Jerrold Ivery
Jerry Blunt
Jerry Boone
Jerry Butler
Jerry Hempfield
Jerry Lyles
Jerry Miller
Jerry W. Lacy
Jesse Armstead
Jesse Hornbuckle
Jesse Jackson
Jesse Johnson

Jesse Lindsey
Jesse Smith
Jessie Nicholson
Jide Shobitan
Jim Brown
Jim Hudson
Jim Kachenmeister
Jim Maddox—
    Congressman
Jim Muse
Jim Raggs
Jim West
Jim Williams
Jimm Cobb
Jimmy R. Toles
Jimmy Walker
Joe (Ovadyau) Ford
Joe Banks
Joe Ford
Joe Harrison
Joe Hunt
Joe Johnson
Joe Parker
Joe Proctor
Joe Williams
Joey Carne
John A. Hopkins
John Arnold
John Bernard
John Bettis
John Blesoe
John Cash
John Chamberlin
John Chapman, Jr.
John Coleman
John Conyers—
    Congressman
John Daniels
John Davis
John Fulbright, III
John Guy
John Howard
John Jackson
John K. Grant, Jr.
John L. Lewis
John L. Russell
John Lewis—
    Congressman
John Little
John McDaniel
John Meyer
John Monds
John Moultrie
John Murchison

John Noxsell
John P. O'Neal
John Posey
John Ratchford
John Richards
John Richmon
John S. Kendall, Esq.
John Scott
John Smooth
John Steele
John Walker
John Washington
John Wayne
John Wesley
John Wilson
Johnathan F.
    Pimental
Johnathan L.
    Williams
Johnathan
    Ratchford
Johnathan Smith
Johnnie Harris
Johnnie Jamison
Johnny B. McCray
Johnny Taylor
Jon Baye
Jon Daye
Jonathan
    McConaughey
Jonathan Parker
Jonathan Pimental
Jonathon Webb
Jordan S. Williams
Jose Jimenez
Joseph Banks
Joseph Evans II
Joseph James
Joseph M. Ovesimus
Joseph Mwandidya
Joseph Rhule
Joseph Twine
Joseph W. Larché, Jr.
Josh Griggs
Joshua Appiah
Joye Carne
Juan Williams
Julian D. Barney
Julian Valentine
Julius A. Jay
Julius Mays
Julius McKinnes
Julius Smith
Juneau Robbins

Justin Cox
Justin Sayles Mann
K. O.
Kahari Walton
Kaine Onwuzulike
Kalum Johnson
Kamal Harris
Kamel Abdo
Kaminsky Thomas
Kappa Alpha Psi
    Fraternity, Inc.
Kareem Coney
Kathy Boyd
Keavin Hutchenson
Kedrick Hogans, Sr.
Keith "From Up the
    Block"
Keith Blaze
Keith Coleman
Keith Cooper
Keith Duncan
Keith Jones
Keith Lucas
Keith McMiller
Keith Ramsey
Keith Rozier
Keith Ruffin
Keith Smith
Keith Washington
Kel Spencer
Ken Brown
Ken Gordon
Ken Hennings
Ken James
Ken Lee
Ken McKay
Ken Rowe
Ken Smikle
Ken Williams
Kendall Steward
Kendall Stewart
Kenneth Barney
Kenneth Brown
Kenneth Carter
Kenneth Chapple
Kenneth Cole
Kenneth Gordon
Kenneth Hodge
Kenneth Lewis
Kenneth Little
Kenneth McGhee
Kenneth Roundtree
Kenneth S. McKay
Kenneth Thomas, Jr.

Kenneth Ward
Kenneth Willis
Kenneth Brown
Kenny Hodge
Kenny McGresham
Kenrick Trapp
Kent
Kenyai Hill
Kervin Clenance
Keven Kenney
Kevin Asford
Kevin Bartholomew
Kevin Brown
Kevin Browning
Kevin C. Meggett
Kevin Davis
Kevin Jones
Kevin K. White
Kevin Kenard
Kevin King
Kevin Mathis
Kevin Mitchell
Kevin Moggett
Kevin Owens
Kevin P. Jones
Kevin Paris
Kevin Patton
Kevin Powell
Kevin S. Harris
Kevin Tannan
Kevin Van Dyke
Khari Walton
Kim Bennett, Chef—
  Soul Café
Kim Houston
Kirk Teasley, Sr.
K'lavell Grayson
Kofi Moyo
Kush Moyo
Kwanza Hall
Kyle Smith
L. C. Felton
Lacey Tyrone Barnes
Lafayette Ford
Lamar Johnson
Lamar R. Sally
Lamont Gray
Lamont "Smiley"
  Moses
Lance Robertson
  Dekalb
Landis Neely
Landon Carter
Lanier Edwards

LaRoy Austin
Larry Bradford
Larry Braxton
Larry Dorney
Larry Gibbs
Larry Green
Larry Lawrence
Larry Lee
Larry Small
Larry Souell
Larry Sowell
Larry Trotter
Larry Tucker
Larry Tuft
Larry W. Robinson
Larry Whitman
Laurence Henry
  Cousins
Lawanda Gordon
Lawrence Head
Lawrence McClellan
Lawrence Simmons
Lawrence Walker
Lawrence Williams
Layfayette Ford
Lee A. Dorris
Lee Bailey
Lee Cohn
Lee D. Valentin
Lee Davis
Lee Richard
Lefton Emenari
Legacy Associates
  Foundation
Leland Atkins
Lemoyne Turner
Lenny Pulliam
Leo Chanoy, Jr.
Leo Jenks, Jr.
Leon Benford
Leon Kirkland
Leon Robinson
Leon Towns
Leon Towns, Sr.
Leonard C. Thomas,
  a.k.a. The Chicken
  Man
Leonard Clark
Leonard Harris
Leonard Johnson,
  M.D.
Leonard Kaigler
Leonard Lawson
Leonard Walker

Leonard Wells
Leroy Bell
Leroy Reynolds
Leroy Summer
Leslie Nance
Leslie Sills
Lester Cornelious
Lester Smith
Lewis Saunders
Lewis Sparks
Lionel Lightbowne
Lionel O. Pittman
Lloyd Roscoe
Lonnie Carter
Lonnie Davis
Lonnie R. Lawrence
Loren B. Chaney
Lorenza Butler II
Lorenzo Bailey
Lorenzo Brown
Lorenzo E. Martin
Lorenzo G. Stacy
Lorenzo Hough
Lorenzo Martin
Lorenzo Spratling
Louis Carr
Louis Dixon
Louis Jones
Louis Theroit
Louis Townsend
Lowell Thomas, Esq.
Lt. Col. Greg
  Galloway
Luis Secaida
Luther A. Campbell
Luther J. Sewell III
Lyle Logan
Lynwood Douthett
Macharia Nhau
Mack Wright
Macon Woodson
Macon Woodson, Jr.
"Magic Man"
Mahiri Anderson
Maia Laville
Mainard Easley
Malcolm Benson
Malcolm Carter
Malcolm Jackson
Malcolm Ratcliffe
Malik Moore
Malik Nevels
Malik Yakini
Mallony D. Jones, III

Marc Campbell
Marc Hodges
Marc Johnson
Marc Williams
Marcel Townsel
Marcel Townsend
Marcelleous Lott
Marco Spoonmark
  Baker
Marcus Stevens
Marcus Webster
Marcy Dnang Fowler
Mario Lemons
Marion Toles
Mark Bartley
Mark Clark
Mark Curry
Mark Fishback
Mark Henderson
Mark Higgs
Mark Jackson
Mark Jones, judge
Mark McLemore
Mark Swinton
Mark Thomas
Markhun Stansbury,
  Jr.
Marrion Heflin
Martel Peguese
Martin Tate
Martye Dixon
Marvin Arrington
Marvin Carter
Marvin Dampier
Marvin Edward
Marvin Johnson
Marvin McNeil
Marvin Neal
Marvin Osborne
Marvin Robinson
Marvin Spruell
Marvin Stewart
Matthew Raiford
Maurice Drake
Maurice Granger
Maurice Thomas
Maurice White
Max Grousse
Mayseo
McKinley Hailey
Mejal K. Dyson
Mel Blackwell
Mel Lemane
Mel Pender

Mell Monroe
Melvin Barnes
Melvin Searles
Melvin Turner
Melvin Wormely
Men of Excellence
Men Who Love
  Larita Shelby@
  Radioscope
Mercer Lawrence
Michael A. Mack,
  Sr.
Michael Arizola
Michael Barney
Michael Bennett
Michael Carney
Michael Childress
Michael Christmas
Michael Crockett
Michael D. "Harpo"
  Bryant
Michael Davis
Michael Flowers
Michael Fountain
Michael Franklin
Michael Goodin
Michael Greer
Michael Hardie
Michael Haynes
Michael Hicks
Michael Hill
Michael Jackson
Michael Jemison
Michael Johnson
Michael Jones
Michael Keeton
Michael Mack, Sr.
Michael MacLenoon
Michael McKinney
Michael Meeks
Michael Mergan
Michael Pinkett
Michael Seay
Michael Simmons
Michael Stephenson
Michael Survet
Michael Swimford
Michael Tracey
Michael Tracy
Michael Vaughn
Michael Wall
Michael Walton
Michael Washington
Michael Watkins

Michael Whitlow
Michael Wilerson
Michael Williams
Mickey Carter
Mickey Rivers
Mike Bruton
Mike Coburn
Mike Johnson
Mike Jones
Mike Love
Mike McCullough
Mike Phillips
Mike Saunders
Miles Jaye
Milton Henderson
Milton Johnson
Milton L. Smith
Milton Morris
Milton Smith
Mitchell Jackson
Modibo "Mo" Keita
Money Wilson
Monroe Anderson
Monte Ford
Monté Fowler
Monty Weddell
Morris F. X. Jeff, Jr.
Morris Nichols
  Gearing
Moses S. Harris
Murdock Thomas
Mylik R. Harrington
Myrna Clayton
Myron H. Walker
N. Charles Anderson
Nafis Ali
Nana Kwesi Oduru
Nate Dyer
Nathaniel Banks
Nathaniel Ryan
Nathaniel
  Thompkins
Ned J. Woods
Nicholas Higgins
Nicholas McCord
Nicholas Spangler
Nicoe Alexander
Nicola Glover
Noah Henry
Noble Reynolds
Nolan R. Harding
Norma Stanley
Norman Coe
Norris Clark

Norwood Clark
O. B. Thomas
Odie Payne III, M.D.
Oliver Mason
Olympia Mel Pender
Omar Leatherman
Omar Stoutmire
Omari A. Brown
Omega Psi Phi
  Fraternity,
  Inc.
Onice Slaughter
Osborn Hurdle
Oscar Smith
Otis Dancy, Jr.
Otis Davis
Otis Henderson
Owen Patterson
Ozzie Baudin
Patrick Amos
Patrick L. Carroll
Patrick Couch
Patrick Fitzsimmons
Patrick Keen
Patrick Obinabo
Patrick Osby
Paul Adams
Paul Alleyene
Paul Freeman
Paul Guiterrez
Paul Johnson
Paul Madyun
Paul Philpott
Paul Riser
Paul Thibodeaux
Paul V. Jordan
Paul Vaughn
Paul Wiltz
Percy Williams
Peryis Hawkins
Pete Shivers
Peter Bynoe
Peter Hamilton
Peter Henderson
Peter Humphries
Peter Martinez
Peter Phillips
Peter Ruiz
Phi Beta Sigma
  Fraternity, Inc.
Phil Powell
Philip Cohn
Phillip Black
Phillip C. Maclin

Phillip Caldwell, II
Phillip Johnson
Phillip Mannuel
Phillip Thigpen
Phillip Washington
Prandal White
Q. Hawkins
Qaid R. Azeez
Que Gaskins
Quentin Franklin
Quentin Love
Quentin Whitelaw
Quest Bass
Raefeael T. Penrice
Raheem Barnes
Rahsaan Gardner
Ral Nwosu
Ralph Harrison
Ralph Jordan
Ralph Metcalfe
Ralph Scott
Ramid Sam
Randal Phillips
Raphael Coleman
Raul Elviro
Ravon Chapman
Ray Anderson
Ray Blackburn
Ray Cojoe, Jr.
Ray Dennis
Ray Glend
Ray Tucker
Raymond Cojoe, Sr.
Raymond Coleman
Raymond Neil
Raymond Silas
Raymond Ward
Rayshun "Shun"
  Dorsey
Reese Price
Reese Quincy Boyd
Reg Jones-Sawyer
Reg Walker
Reggie Bulger
Reggie Carter
Reggie Rhodes
Reginald Butler
Reginald A. Wilon
Reginald Carpenter
Reginald Greenlee
Reginald Jones-
  Sawyer
Reginald L. Cohill
Reginald Ray

Reginald Rush
Reginald Sigler
Reginald Speers
Reid King
Reuben M. Brown
Rev. Donald
Gatewood
Rev. Jim Lee
Rev. Kenneth Lamar
Jones
Rev. Leslie Davis
Rev. Tyrone A.
Patton
Rex Marshall
Ricardo Johnson
Ricardo Villanosa
Richard A. Cruz
Richard Bailey
Richard Barney
Richard Blackmon
Richard Blackmon
III
Richard Blackmon,
Jr.
Richard Bradford
Richard Gary
Richard Horton
Richard Lee Snow
Richard Mays
Richard Muhammad
Richard Newhouse
Richard P. Mays
Richard Pannell
Richard Petty
Richard Richter
Richard Steele
Rick Holton
Ricky Fields
Ricky McKenzie
Ricky White
Rigoberto Elviro
R. J. Speaks
Rob Jon
Robert A. Burns
Robert Bennett
Robert Bouya
Robert C. Anderson
Robert Cole
Robert D. Garland
Robert E. Brown
Robert Edison
Robert Green
Robert I. Johnson
Robert J. Johnson

Robert Jackson
Robert James
Robert James, M.D.
Robert Johnson
Robert L. Haynes
Robert Lort
Robert Mays
Robert McReynolds
Robert Morris,
Owner—Peaches
& Cream Café
Robert O'Brian
Robert Patrick
Robert Polk
Robert Thunderbird
Robin Robinson
Rock Fraire
Rockney Carter
Rod Booker
Roderick Rischer
Roderick Sawyer
Roderick Smith
Roderick Taylor
Roderick White
Rodney Baltimore
Rodney Brown
Rodney H. Pate
Rodney Hill
Rodney K. Whitaker
Rodney Pate
Rodney Smith
Rodney Vance
Rodney Von
Johnson
Rodney Wearry
Rodrick Clarke
Roger Jackson
Roger L. Paden
Roger L. Poden
Roger Short
Roger Thomas
Roger V. Thomas
Roland McFarlane
Roland S. Martin
Romy Vasquez
Ron Allen
Ron Atkins
Ron Bolden
Ron Hill
Ron Legrand
Ron Lyles
Ron Miller
Ron Montgomery
Ron Oliney

Ron Saine
Ron Turner
Ron Wilson
Ronald Barr
Ronald Bell
Ronald Buford
Ronald C. Sandidge,
Sr.
Ronald Johnson
Ronald McFadden
Ronald Miller
Ronald Perry
Ronald Perryman
Ronald Smith
Ronald Washington
Ronald Williams
Ronnell Smith
Ronnie Arch
Ronnie Devoe
Ronnie Wilson
Roosevelt Gaines
Roosevelt McGee
Roosevelt Moncure
Roosevelt Myles
Rori Blakeney
Roy Blackburn
Roy F. Williams
Roy Foster
Roy Gifford
Roy Jones, Jr.
Roy Robinson
Ruben Brown
Rudolph Jackson
Rudy Jones
Rudy Rush
Rudy S. Goodwine
Rufus Jonson
Russ Schellenger
Russell Bezdek
Russell Gilliam
Russell Ricks
Ryan Thibodeaux
Sabir Majeed
Saiden Brown
Sam Grenshaw
Sam Hill
Sam McGrier
Sam Robinson
Sam Walker
Sammie Clark
Sammy Ngera
Samuel Akinmulero
Samuel Bacote
Samuel Lawrence

Samuel Varnado
San Esake
Sanford
Scott A. Phillips
Scott Chaney
Scott D. Robinson
Scott Daniels
Sean Hicks
Sedrick Brass
Seitu Hayden
Sekar Shorter
Seneferu Kephra
Seutter Swan
Shabazz Rahim
Shaffdeen A. Amuwo
Shane Price
Shannon Faulk
Shannon Hamilton
Shawl Pryor
Shawn Conway
Shawn Lewis
Shedrick Sawyer
Sheldon B. Ross
Shelton Allwood
Shelton Stoker
Sidney King
Sidney Sealy, Sr.
Sigmund "OJ" Smith
Sir Ravon Chapman
Smokin' Kevin
Solomon Nixon
Sonny Smith
Sporty King
Stan Perkins
Stedman Graham
Stefan Jordan
Steffan Cooks
Steffon D. Josey
Stephen Carter
Stephen Jackson
Stephen L. Carter, Sr.
Stephen Limbrick
Stephen Maybank
Foster
Stephen Whitehead
Sterling Ingram
Steve Allen
Steve Braxton
Steve C. Bluford
Steve Farmer
Steve Honeyman
Steve L. Wesley
Steve Watkins
Steve White

Steve. C. Bluford
Steven McKinney
Steven Stanley
Steven Swartz
Steven Wakins
Stevie Smith
Stinson Brown
Swieliang Tan
Sylvester Taylor
T. X. T. Jahnes
Taiwan Singleton
Tamlin Henry
Tanto Irie
Tanya Hill
Taquaan B. El-Amin
Tarik Scott
Tavis Hunter
Ted Crowder
Terrance Davis
Terrence Jackson
Terretta Scope
Terrill Hill
Terry Allen
Terry Cousin
Terry Muhammad
Terry Toliver
Terry Wayne Owens
Terry Whitfield
Terryon Jefferson
Thabiti Cartman,
  M.D.
Thaddeus Dodson
Thaddeus L. Wilson
Thaddeus Wilson
Theodore Coleman
Theodore Crowder
Thom Rivers
Thomas Ely
Thomas Finch
Thomas Fuller,
  congressman
Thomas J. Elliot
Thomas P. Hixon
Thomas Randall
Thomas Rashid
Thomas Sampson
Thomas Triplett
Tiffany Anderson
Tiffany Cochran
Tim Dillinger
Tim Reid
Tim Richardson
Tim Taylor
Tim Thompson

Timothy A. Turner
Timothy Pete
Timothy Smith
Timothy Turner
Tito Staten
Tommy DeLoach
Tommy Harris
Tony B.
Tony Bolton
Tony Gabriel
Tony Glover
Tony Moore
Tony Navarro
Tony Nixon
Torrance Brown
Torrence Brown
Toure Muhammad
Travis Jackson
Travis L. Williams
Trizelle Jenkins
Trojan A. Jackson
Troy Edmond
Troy Jackson
Troy Maurice
  Williams
Turane William
Turtel Onli
Tyrone Backers
Tyrone Belcher
Tyrone Bynum
Tyrone Smith
Tyrone Tucker
Undrae Winding
Valerie Sholes
Van Isaacs
Vance C. Roux
Vance T. Kimber
Vassie Lee Hill
Vaughn Woods
Vernell Cox
Vernon Caldwell
Vernon Martin
Vernon McLean
Vester Hudson
Victor Armendaris
Victor Chears
Victor Cheatman
Victor Cheatman, Jr.
Victor Golden
Victor McLean
Vince Bradford
Vincent A. Hawk
Vincent A. Hubbard
Vincent Craig

## Michael Stallworth, president, Organized Black Men, Inc.

For the past nine years, Michael has helped Real Men Cook by recruiting a team of men to join us. The purpose of his organization is to connect with young people (ages twelve through seventeen) and mentor them. "I like to bring the kids along to the event so that they can see the positive role models. We teach these kids by showing them what real men are all about. It's not about the food—it's all about the kids, especially the ones who don't have positive reinforcement in their lives," says Stallworth. Michael's dedication to working with the kids and at our event demonstrates his devotion to the philosophy of Real Men Cook. Carry on, brother!

—K.K.M.

Vincent Reyes
Virgil Fludd
W. John Mitchell
Waddell Brent
Wade McCree, judge
Wade Patterson
Walt Whitman, Jr.
Walter Cannon
Walter D. Space
Walter Payton
Walter Richardson
Walter Whitman
Warren Cooper
Warren Hutcherson
Warren Savage
Warren Williams
Waukegan Real Men
  Cook
Wayne C. Watson
Wayne Elliot Sheats

Wayne Jefferson
Wayne Sheats
Wayne Watson
Weller Thomas
Wendell (Tex)
  Wilson
Wendell Killitte
Wendell Kimbrough
Wendell R. Fields
Wendell Wilson
Wesley K. Cooper
Whitfield Jones
Wil Lucas
Wilbert Baber, Jr.
Wiley A. Warren
Wilfred Harris
Will Ali
William Allen
William Alfred
  Sampson, M.D.

William Andrews
William Bernstein II
William Coit
William E. Keene
William G. Taylor
William Gerstein
William J. Williams
William Jones
William Knight
William Leonard
  Harris

William Lewis
William McClellan,
  Jr.
William McCormick
William McCray
William Murphy
William Mustafa
William Sampson
William Tucker
Willie Ali
Willie Anderson

Willie L. Anderson
Willie E. Keeler
Willie Hooker
Willie J. Osborne
Willie King
Willie L. Berry
Willie Nash
Willie Scott
Willie Toombs
Willie Wright
Willis A. Harris

Wilson Perisee
Windsor Jordan
Winfield Pettaway
Xavier C. Gordon
Yom Siem
Yorel Frances
Yosheyah Moyo
Yves Thony
Zac Covington
Zahdok Levi
Zee Bradford

# Acknowledgments

Special thanks to my wife and business partner, Yvette; together we have endured continuing challenges and changes in every imaginable way, some too painful to recount here. Much of what Real Men Cook has become is due to her dedication during some incredible hours of attention to detailed work on the national campaign to change the way Father's Day is celebrated, and the elevation and recognition of the role of fathers in family and community.

I would be remiss indeed if I did not acknowledge and thank the other women behind the Real Men who cook. The list includes Dr. Carol Adams, now director of the Illinois Department of Human Services; Eunice Chaney, public relations professional (now deceased); Deborah Crable, radio personality and television producer; Merri Dee, television host and station executive; Michelle Flowers, advertising entrepreneur; Tanya Hill, advertising professional; Kim Houston, former Real Men Cook staff; Debra Jury, manager, hotel and resort industry; Leslye Logan, public school teacher; Greta Miller, former RMC staff; Robin Robinson, news anchor; Carolyn Shelton, food specialist; Jennifer Schultz, sales and event coordinator; Lucinda Doles White, health consultant; and Martha Worrell, theater executive and consultant. These fifteen women provided the foundation of volunteer support without which Real Men Cook would never have survived to become the event it is today.

In December 2001, during an oftimes annual hiatus to St. Thomas, in the U.S. Virgin Islands, visitation and hospitality provided by lifelong friend and spiritual brother Dr. J. Fletcher Robinson, I began the narrative that comprises the body of this work. Fletcher is a "struggling to retire" dermatologist who just can't wait to get rid of the necessity of practicing medicine in order to get on with his traveling, collecting African art, being curator/librarian of his many collections of books on black writers, painters, and photographers, and daily hosting a meeting place for a large number of expatriate professionals from the mainland who have found a degree of paradise among the living. Late in life Fletcher is taking an active role in maintaining the history of great cooks and their recipes from his own childhood. However, whenever I am there, I become chief cook and bottle washer in order to earn my keep. I am eternally grateful for your friendship, Fletcher. Thank you!

Many times during the past three years I have retreated to Savannah, to the home of Dr. Mark Stewart, his wife, Lauren, and girls Sidney and Taylor, where I sought refuge from the rigors of business and time to continue to review, edit, and rewrite the hundreds of hours of taped interviews, hours taken with the men who have filled me with the appreciation and expanded notion of who these men are. Savannah is very close to the Sea Islands, off the South Carolina coast, a very protected and spiritual place in the history of the forced immigration of Africans to North America; I found a very inspirational venue from which to write.

Rudy Lombard, author of *Creole Feast: 15 Master Chefs of New Orleans Reveal Their Secrets* and a close friend of Fletcher Robinson, added significant counsel to my early search for direction and scope of what I wanted to do. Rudy, like a good roux, brought together many of the elements of history and contemporary thought regarding food and food preparation.

A long period of discussion, book reading, attending others' book release parties, and general procrastination ended at the insistence of Donna Beasley, author and children's book publisher: "Kofi, some people are wannabees, some gonnabees, and then there are the gottabees." Thanks, Donna!

The following names are those that I can remember as I become numb and my deadline approaches like the forces of nature meeting in a whirlwind. Chaga Walton tried to help me with the interviews early on, until he found me just a little "over the top"; thirty plus years we have been on this path together—don't stop now! Haki Madhubuti, Paul Coats (Third World Press), Karon Hamlet (Classic Black Press), Visions Blu, there at the beginning (writer), Marsha Braddix (transcription), Sharon Morgan (writer, chef, and more), Wilbert Jones (author and writer), Victor Powell (photographer and computer graphics guru), Eric Futran (food photographer), Chef Kocoa Wimbush (food stylist), Charla Draper (food stylist), Chef Michael Seay of All Seasons, Inc., Chef Basil Brathwaite, Laurie Saunders (Albertson's, Jewel-Osco), Wynona Redmond (Dominick's Finer Foods), Sherwin Wilner (Isaacson & Stein Fish Company), Leonard and Donna Harris (Chatham Food Center), Felton Armand (Advance Information Resources—keeping our computers online), Maya James (help when it counts), Kim Jeff, Roshinda Evans, Jamal Oliver (Works in Progress), Cynthia Jordan (Royal Affairs), Laura Dyson (seamstress), Kenneth Hennings (Best Chef Products), Pam Rice and Beth D'anado (writers), Lisa Skirloff (public relations), Linda Konnor (agent), Fran Bell (South Side YMCA), Susan Peters and Tara Jackson and Amita Jackson (Real Men Cook staff), Cynthia Stringfellow (moral support), Rudolph and Pauline Jackson. Along with those mentioned above are legions of male and female volunteers who are our operational base for the event on Father's Day, so many nameless yet essential parts of who and what we have become.

On the Internet, dhfinecuisine@aol.com is where you will find the email connection to the electric personality of Donna Hodge, journalist, foodie, photographer, author, event planner, producer, and the person responsible for making *Real Men Cook: Rites, Rituals, and Recipes for Living* a reality. Now that we work in a virtual world of faxes and email, what a comfort it has been to know that a real person is at the other end of the message, someone sensitive enough to interpret the intent and meaning of the messenger. Thank you, Donna!

To Cherise Davis, my editor at Simon & Schuster, words are insufficient to express my gratitude for allowing me the opportunity to share that voice of Real Men Cook, Real Men Love, Real Men Care, Real Men Provide, Real Men Work, Real Men Build, Real Men Become Fathers of Real Men.

# Special acknowledgments:

Chatham Food Center
The Chicago Smoke House
Isaacson & Stein Fish Company
R. J. Dale Advertising, Albertson—Jewel-Osco
Flowers Communications, Lawry's Brands
Safeway-Dominick's Finer Foods
Mel and Angela Monroe, "The Abundance Table"
B.J.'s Market & Bakery—Chef Jon Meyer

# Real Men Cook® Merchandise

## Apparel

**Black Cotton Apron** with African print design on the pockets and at the neck. Chef's hat crown is matching African print with black hatband. Apron and hat are imprinted with the Real Men Cook® logo, with or without the Father's Day panel. Your choice of red or white lettering.

Set of apron and hat, $40.00. Hat, $20.00. Apron, $25.00.

Real Men Cook® Logo T-shirts

Long-sleeved mock turtleneck. Black or white. Your choice of red or white lettering. Sizes small to XL, $20.00; 2X and 3X, $25.00.

Short-sleeved black or white shirts with logo, imprinted in your choice of red or white. Sizes small to 3X, $15.00.

Real Men Cook® baseball caps.

Flame design with red lettering, black or white, adjustable to fit all sizes, $15.00.

## Foods

Real Men Cook Sweet Potato Pound Cake® Mix, $3.00. Case of 12, $30.00.

Real Men Cook® (Special Recipe) Hot Sauce, 2 ounces, $3.00. Case of 24, $65.00.

## Books

*Real Men Cook: Rites, Rituals, and Recipes for Living;* signed copies, in some cases by author *and* contributing cooks.

Bulk orders available at significant discounts; visit www.realmencook.com

Limited supply, collectors issues of past annual commemorative books (*Tips, Quips, and Recipes from Real Men Cook*) from the past fifteen years (when available): years 1–5, $15.00 per issue; 6–10, 11–15, all or any combination, $3.00 per issue.

All orders of $50.00 or more will receive two Real Men Cook® refrigerator magnets free while supplies last!

Packing, shipping, and guaranteed delivery, $5.95 minimum; $25.01–$50.00/$9.00; $50.01–$75.00/$12.00; $75.01–$150.00/$16.00; $150.01–$300.00/$20.00.

Please allow 6 to 8 weeks for delivery.

Nationally, the Real Men Cook Sweet Potato Pound Cake® mix can be purchased at Albertson's, Cub, Safeway, and other select supermarket chains. Ask your grocer for the product by name, Real Men Cook Sweet Potato Pound Cake.

A percentage of all net proceeds from the sale of Real Men Cook® products goes to support Real Men Charities, Inc., a nonprofit 501(c)3 organization.

# Index